Understanding Government Finance

Brian Romanchuk

Published by BondEconomics, Canada

www.BondEconomics.com

Paperback edition published by BondEconomics, 2016, Montréal Québec.

Nothing in this book constitutes investment or tax advice. Investors are advised to seek professional advice tailored to their situation. Although best efforts have been made to ensure the validity of information contained herein, there is no guarantee of its accuracy or completeness.

Cover Image: John Tyo 5¢ Token, 1895. National Currency Collection, Currency Museum, Bank of Canada. Used with permission.

Library and Archives Canada
Understanding government finance
Brian Romanchuk 1968-
ISBN 978-0-9947480-0-3 Epub Edition (June 2015)
ISBN 978-0-9947480-1-0 Kindle Edition (June 2015)
ISBN 978-0-9947480-5-8 Paperback Edition

Contents

List of Figures

Acknowledgements

I would like to thank the readers of my articles at BondEconomics.com for their feedback. Portions of this text previously appeared as articles on that site, and I have been able to incorporate suggestions and corrections. I have noted particular contributions within the endnotes of this document. I would also like to thank Leo Kolivakis and Tom McConville for their feedback on my manuscript.

I would also like to thank Judy Yelon for her editing of this text.

Finally, any errors and omissions are my own.

Chapter 1 Overview

1.1 Introduction

One often hears the suggestion that a central government's budget is just like that of a household or a corporation. Although it is true that double-entry bookkeeping applies to governments as well as households, any resemblance is largely superficial and misleading. A central government defines the nature of the monetary system in which it operates, which is not the case for those in the private sector. The limits of government spending are not determined by narrow financial constraints, but rather, its effects on the broader economy. After all, no other entity can legally print money!

There are two common conventional arguments as to why governments face financial constraints. The first is that the bond market could refuse to lend to the government, which is known as *rollover risk*. The second form of constraint is based on arguments from economic theory, known as the *governmental budget constraint*. This report discusses these concepts, and explains why they do not appear to bind governments.

This freedom from financial constraints does not characterise *all* governments. A government that fixes its currency to an external instrument, or a sub-sovereign government (a city, province or state) faces financial constraints due to this lack of control over its financing. This report is not aimed at the analysis of such governments, although there is some discussion of how they differ from governments lacking such constraints. Examples of governments that I will be discussing are the central (federal) governments of countries such as Canada, the United States, the United Kingdom, Japan, and Australia.

This report is aimed at those who have an interest in governmental finance, but who are not necessarily experts. The use of equations is largely avoided; instead, concepts are illustrated with graphs. The focus is on the operations behind government finance, and so there is limited discussion of economic theory. This reduces the scope of discussion, an analysis of the specific effects of fiscal policy upon the economy requires the use of economic theory.

The focus here is upon the general principles of governmental finance, and not the details of its accounting nor the financial mechanics. Towards this end, a Simplified Framework of governmental finance is developed and explained. This framework is quite similar to current Canadian practices.

Although the objective is to avoid discussing economic theory in detail, some of the basic concepts of Modern Monetary Theory (MMT) are introduced. Modern Monetary Theory is a school of thought within post-Keynesian economics, which is distinguished by its focus on the operations used in government finance. This book is within the MMT tradition, but I am not attempting to make this an introduction to all of the concepts used by MMT. I am presenting the analysis of governmental finance in a conventional manner, and I am discussing a framework in which bank reserves do not exist. (Many of the existing primers on MMT are couched in terms of a system that uses bank reserves.) Once the underlying principles are understood, bank reserves can be bolted onto the framework as a special case.

I would also note that I am trying to follow a neutral analytical stance, but my message will probably not be welcomed by fiscal conservatives (who tend to be the ones that argue that the government budget is just like a household budget). In my view, this is just laziness on their part; it is entirely possible to argue in favour of a smaller government without inventing non-existent financial constraints on fiscal policy. In any event, the intended audience includes those with an interest in the bond markets, and these readers will eventually discover that investment strategies that rely upon financial constraints biting into governments with free-floating currencies are almost certain money-losers.

I am not proposing any particular set of reforms to the monetary system (other than arguing that the financial system ought to be properly regulated). By contrast, there is a large number of people arguing for deep reforms to the monetary system, which is a reaction to the shenanigans that became apparent during the Financial Crisis of 2007-2009. (Throughout this text, I refer to that particular financial crisis as "the Financial Crisis," which may appear quaint if other intervening crises appear by the time you are reading this.) Although I am well aware of the defects of the current system, I believe that the reforms need to be focussed on the real economy, not the monetary system.

1.2 About this Report

This report is the first one published by BondEconomics.com. Later reports will cover other topics of interest in the analysis of bond markets and monetary economics. The target audience will vary from report-to-report, as will the level of complexity.

This report is aimed at those who are not specialists, but who are comfortable reading media articles about finance or economics. The amount of jargon being used has been reduced, although some technical terms are retained if they are commonly used elsewhere, and an explanation is given. This text is not aimed at academics, and no attempt has been made to provide an exhaustive literature survey. The references supplied should allow an interested reader to begin developing a more formal understanding of the literature if so desired.

This report was first published as an ebook (an eReport) in 2015. Small changes have been made to the text to reflect the differences in format.

I finally wish to note that this report uses Canadian spelling and punctuation, which is a hybrid between English and American customs. The most obvious difference here is my use of *cheque* rather than the American *check*. I keep American spelling unchanged within quotations, as well as in proper names (such as Hyman Minsky's book, *Stabilizing an Unstable Economy*, which I would render as *Stabilising*).

Montréal, Canada, June 2015.
(Paperback edition prepared in June 2016.)

Chapter 2 Understanding Money

2.1 Introduction

This report is a discussion of monetary operations and government finance in contemporary developed economies, in which the value of the currency floats freely. At the time of writing, the only developed economies where the currency is not free-floating are those within the euro area, and other nations that are closely linked to the euro (for example, Denmark). However, the situation is fluid, and it is possible that some or all of those countries will have free-floating currencies by the time you read this.

My starting point is how the monetary system works, and I am not discussing what economists refer to as the "real economy"–the production of goods and services. To offer an example of what this distinction means, I am not discussing what resource inputs are required to produce 10,000 automobiles, rather I am discussing how those automobiles are paid for.

This is a departure from conventional textbooks, where one starts with a simplified "real economy," where exchanges consist of barter. (A *barter* transaction is one in which goods and services are exchanged without money–or a claim on money–being exchanged.) It is only in later chapters that a special good–money–is introduced.

In my view, this barter-based theoretical framework is misleading and unhelpful. The normal assumption is that goods are valued in barter transactions on how much "utility" they provide when they are consumed. For example, if you prefer to eat a banana rather than an apple, you would be happy to trade an apple for a banana. Although this works for goods that are consumed, money is not directly consumed (except when rich people light cigars with high denomination notes as a form of conspicuous consumption). This then forces economists to insert any number of "fixes" into their models to explain why money has value.

2.2 Money Is a Unit of Account

If we are analysing a monetary economy, the first question to ask is: "What is money?"

Some economists can give a very long answer to that question. However, from the perspective of someone analysing the monetary operations of a modern economy, the best answer is: *money is a unit of account.*

In other words, money is a unit of measurement, not a thing in itself. Like a kilogram, for instance. You can have a kilogram of feathers, you can have a kilogram of breakfast cereal, you can even have a standard kilogram weight, but you cannot have "a kilogram."

If a kilogram measures mass, what does money measure? It measures debt.

All forms of money in a modern economy are effectively debt instruments, and monetary transactions therefore consist of a trade of something else for a debt instrument. These debt instruments are measured in a common unit, which is the domestic currency like the Canadian dollar, U.S. dollar, or the British pound.

If there were no common unit of measure, it would be extremely difficult to pay these debts back. This is because debts are often settled by the debtor handing the lender a debt instrument of a third party, and you need a common measure to compare their values.

The creation of this unit of account also allows double-entry bookkeeping to function.

For example, a corner store can have many different goods in inventory: the amounts of types of chocolate bars, drinks, etc. The storeowner has to track this "real" inventory, and call suppliers to replenish particular products as they are sold. However, if that storeowner has a loan with a bank, the bank will wish to see accounting statements with the amount of inventory, so that the bank can judge the health of the business. The banker does not want to see a list of each type of chocolate bar, rather a one-line summary like "Inventory: $10,000". The only way to lump together all of the various types of inventory is to assign each of them a monetary value, and then aggregate (add up) those values.

If we want to analyse a monetary economy, we need to analyse the interactions of the balance sheets (and income statements) of all the entities within that economy. Like the storeowner, we can only aggregate all these different activities by looking at their monetary values. Roughly speaking, the sum of all monetary incomes within a domestic economy (that is, excluding income earned overseas by nationals) is Gross Domestic Income, which equals (within measurement errors) the more commonly used Gross

Domestic Product (GDP).

From the point of view of modelling the economy, it does not normally appear to matter what the medium of monetary transactions is. Whether transactions are concluded with the exchange of promises-to-pay (such as electronic transfers) or silver coins, does not normally matter. The time when the form of money becomes important is when there are restrictions upon its availability.

Figure 1. *John Tyo Token (Currency Museum, Bank of Canada)*

The British North American colonies (that later merged to form Canada) provided an example of how commerce had to work around a shortage of money. These colonies were somewhat indifferently managed from London, and there was a continuous shortage of copper currency (pennies and halfpennies). This shortage led various businesses to issue tokens, which then circulated. The image in Figure 1 is an example of a token issued in 1895 by John Tyo, the owner of a hotel (photo credit[1]). The quality of tokens was quite uneven, and they were sometimes issued without any official sanction.

The one penny token in Figure 2[2] was issued in 1837 in Lower Canada (which became Québec) by the Québec Bank. This was part of a larger issue of bank tokens which replaced those issued by non-banks, as those non-bank tokens were of quite low quality (for example, brass was used instead of

Figure 2. *Québec Bank Token.*

---

1   John Tyo 5¢ Token, 1895. National Currency Collection, Currency Museum, Bank of Canada. Used with permission.

2   Photo credit: Brian Romanchuk.

copper).[3]

In the modern era, there is no longer a shortage of coinage for commerce. However, there is an imbalance in the desire for safe money market instruments versus their supply. The demand was created by the rise of money market funds, which drew money away from the formal banking system. This has led investment bankers to be quite creative in their ability to designate securities as being "money-like" instruments. This creativity has led to various financial crises since the mid-1960s, culminating in the rather spectacular meltdown in the money markets during the Financial Crisis.

Although this tendency of the private sector to create new forms of money in order to grease the wheels of commerce is an important economic force, it does not have a direct impact on governmental finance. Correspondingly, private sector money creation is not pursued further here.

2.3 Chartalism

Chartalism is a school of thought within economics that views money as being inherently tied to the nation-state. Chartalism (sometimes spelled Cartalism) has a long history, but is now prominent because Modern Monetary Theory (MMT) has adopted a streamlined version of the framework. As a result, MMT is sometimes referred to as *Neo-Chartalist*. This is discussed within other works by MMT authors, such as *Understanding Modern Money* by L. Randall Wray.

There is some controversy around Chartalism with respect to the history of money. The theory is disputed by those who advocate gold-backed money, as they argue that gold was money without any state backing. In my view, Chartalism describes the present situation quite well; whether or not this was always true is not germane to this report. This topic is covered in detail within the previously mentioned book by L. Randall Wray.

The bulk of money used within an economy is private; such as deposits in the banking system. Theoretically, there is little reason that these private debts are denominated in the same unit of account as the government. Businesses may use a foreign currency; commonly the United States dollar. Furthermore, there have been attempts to launch purely private cur-

---

3   My comments here are based upon historical details provided in *Canadian Colonial Tokens (Eighth Edition)*, by W.K. Cross, The Charlton Press, 2012.

rencies, such as Bitcoin. There is considerable trading activity in gold and silver coins, which some view as a form of private money. However, in the developed world, these precious metal coins are generally not used in commerce.

The following questions then arise.

- Why does the private banking sector normally denominate accounts in the government-issued currency?
- Why does government money hold value, when it is issued in inherently worthless paper or non-precious metals, or even just electronic entries?

The Chartalist answer is that this is primarily the result of taxes. Taxes create the demand for currencies, which would otherwise have no value in exchange. Legal strictures such as legal tender laws are viewed to be of secondary importance. For example, I am unaware of any cases of Canadian firms being charged under legal tender laws, despite the widespread acceptance of United States dollars at retail firms.

Examples of how taxes and other institutional factors cause the governmental currency to drive out other units of account are listed below.

- Businesses need to acquire the state currency to pay income tax and Value Added Tax (VAT) liabilities. If revenues came in the form of other currencies, they need to exchange them continuously for the state currency.
- Even if businesses and individuals engage in barter transactions, they are *supposed* to treat the barter transaction as a pair of monetary transactions, which are then declared as taxable income (and for VAT purposes). This creates the need to acquire state currency in order to meet the tax obligation.
- A significant portion of worker salaries is deducted at source. This creates demand for state currency at each pay period.
- Income tax preparation would be difficult if pay was given in a different currency. All pay would have to be converted at the exchange rates prevailing at the time.
- Accounting and risk hedging is difficult in a multi-currency system.
- Most entities within the economy are already enmeshed in a web of debt obligations denominated in the state currency. If

you have a mortgage denominated in the state currency that represents a good portion of your after-tax income, a salary in another currency is a risky proposition.

These factors create a large barrier to entry for rival domestic units of account.

2.4 Money and Bonds

The money and bond markets are intertwined; using financial market terminology, you can think of bonds as "forward money." If you use a strict definition of money–such as dollar bills–money does not pay interest. (A twenty-dollar bill is always worth twenty dollars.) As a result, people wish to find alternative instruments that pay interest, yet keep a steady value. (Stocks are expected to rise in value and pay dividends, but their value is quite unstable.) The more stable the price of the instrument, the closer it is to "money."

The most common way of earning interest on money is to leave it on deposit at a bank. Before central banks lost their way and slashed their policy rates to near zero, savings accounts used to pay interest. Additionally, one can have a term deposit at a bank, which typically pays a higher rate of interest–at the cost of tying up your money for a longer period of time.

From the perspective of someone in the private sector, a *bond* is just an alternative to a bank term deposit. Instead of lending money to a bank for a fixed period, you lend to the issuer of the bond. (*Issuer* is the usual term for borrowers in the bond market.) The only distinction between a bond and an ordinary loan is that bonds are securities that can be traded to others. (The initial issuance of the bond is called the *primary market*; the later trading occurs on the *secondary market*.) This makes bonds subject to securities regulations. Given the costs to set up a bond, they are typically only available to large borrowers (or by pooling together small loans within *securitisations*).

One important reason why investors wish to earn interest with bonds is to make up for the loss of purchasing power of money due to inflation. Within a capitalist economy, prices are continuously rising and falling. In order to discern a pattern of price movements, statisticians calculate price indices that are some form of average of a number of prices. The most well known is the Consumer Price Index (CPI), but there are a number of other measures that are used. Inflation is a steady rise in these price indices. The mainstream consensus is that central banks can control the level of inflation with interest rate policy, and in some countries, the central bank has a formal target for inflation. (For example, the Bank of Canada aims to keep the annual rate of inflation near 2%.) The topic of inflation is discussed further within Chapter 7.

The payments associated with the bond are the *principal payment*, and the *coupon payments*. The principal payment is normally made at the maturity of the bond. (In some cases, principal payments are made earlier, although those bonds are typically issued by the private sector. This is similar to residential mortgage payments, where a part of the principal is paid down as part of every mortgage payment.) The coupon payments are specified as a percentage of the principal; for example, if you buy a piece of a bond with a 5% coupon where the principal payment is $100, the bond pays $5 in coupon payments every year over the lifetime of the bond (including the year of maturity). In some countries, coupon payments are typically made only once per year (annual coupons), while others have the convention that bonds pay one-half of the coupon rate every six months (semi-annual coupons).

The more you pay for a bond, the lower the implied interest rate on your investment (termed the bond yield). Since you are always receiving the same payments back from the bond, the more you pay, the less you get relative to your investment. "Price up, yield down (and vice-versa)." This is discussed further in Appendix 1. Bond investors spend their days contemplating bond prices and economic data, hoping to guess which bonds will have the best price performance over the next few days or months.

From the perspective of a bond investor, a central government bond appears pretty much like a bond issued by any other entity. However, when we take the perspective of borrowers, the central government has a very different view on bond issuance when compared with others. The difference between their outlooks is the subject of the later chapters of this report.

From the perspective of a bond investor, there are three risks associated with bond ownership.

1. Bond yields could rise, reducing the value of the bond. (This is known as *interest rate risk*.) An introduction to what factors determine bond yields is given in Sections 6.2-6.5.
2. The issuer of the bond may not be able to make its contractually

obligated payments (or refuse to do so). This is known as default risk, and in the case of a central government, this is typically referred to as *rollover risk*. This is the subject of Section 6.6.

3.   There is the question of *inflation risk*–will the payments received be worth less than expected, because prices have risen? An introduction to the topic of inflation is found in Section 7.2.

The mechanics of the bond market will be the subject of other reports published by *BondEconomics.com*, but some introductory material is found in the sections noted above. The analysis of this report is largely based on the point of view of an issuing government, and so the mechanics of how private sector investors trade the bonds amongst themselves does not really matter. The key point for the purpose of this report is that the private sector trades off holding bonds versus holding money.

2.5 Concluding Remarks

Although the private sector can and does issue money of various types, the central government in modern economies forces a standardisation towards the money it issues for when it deals with the public. This includes money defined within the banking system, where the government gives the banks special privileges in exchange for the banks facing a stricter regulatory regime than the rest of the financial system. The effect of this is to standardise the unit of account within a country to be the central government's money, and not a private sector unit of account. Government bonds are purchased by the private sector to replace money (which pays no interest) with a security that earns interest.

Chapter 3 Introduction to Government Finances

3.1 Introduction

An emphasis on government financial operations is one of the distinguishing features of Modern Monetary Theory (MMT). The importance of financial operations is that they implicitly act as a constraint on the possible set of transactions.

Topics of discussion where an understanding of operations is important are listed below.

- How can governments pay for their programmes when they run fiscal deficits?
- If the government borrows money, does that borrowing "crowd out" private sector activity?
- Does government borrowing raise interest rates?
- What is the difference between sovereign borrowers that have run into problems–most recently, Greece–and other sovereigns?
- Do foreign owners of government bonds have the power to dictate policies to governments?
- How does a country with a fixed exchange rate or a fixed gold parity[4] differ from a country with a freely floating currency?

I am not going to attempt to answer all of these questions within this report, as these are complex topics, and there is no consensus about the answers. Instead, I offer the preceding list to explain why operations matter and I will outline my thinking on some of these topics in the remainder of this text.

3.2 Constraints within Economic Models

There are many broad ways to approach the study of economics, but what I wish to discuss here are approaches that are based upon either implicit or explicit mathematical models.

[4]   A gold parity is a fixed price for which a government exchanges its currency for gold. These were a defining feature of the Gold Standard, and continued its existence until the United States "closed the Gold Window."

We often look at monthly or quarterly economic data, either real world data from statistical agencies or data from a simulated economy. We want to be able to build relationships between these time series. Obviously, the relationships in real world economies are very complex, so we often want to think about them in terms of simplified models, as it is difficult to grasp the interrelationships of a highly complex system.

Within these economic models, there are three types of rules that govern the behaviour of variables. In mathematics as well as economics, these can be known as constraints, as they constrain the relationships between the variables. (Absent constraints, any set of trajectories could be a solution to a problem, which makes the mathematical model useless for providing guidance.) The classes are:

1. accounting identities;
2. behavioural rules;
3. the set of feasible transactions.

The set of accounting relationships amongst all of the entities within an economy is important, as they determine what types of economic outcomes are possible. If a household is paid a wage that is saved at a bank, the household's bank balance should rise by the amount saved. An economic model would not be useful if such accounting relationships break down.

However, accounting rules are not enough to determine how an economy, or a model of an economy, behaves. Although all models should agree what happens to your bank account when you save $10, different models may generate wildly different predictions about the percentage of your income that you will save.[5] Therefore, behavioural rules are critical.

The importance of the first two types of rules has long been recog-

---

5   This is discussed in greater length in Section 4.6.5 (The Limits of SFC Accounting) in Marc Lavoie's *Post-Keynesian Economics: New Foundations* (note: SFC refers to "stock-flow consistent"). "While it may be relatively easy to agree on the main structural features of a simplified economy, different economists see the behaviour of firms or banks and even households in many different ways… Thus the results obtained with these different models will differ, as has been confirmed when new SFC models, with assumptions slightly different than from those earlier ones, produced different trajectories. But this provides for lively discussions!" (pp. 273-274).

nised, while the constraints created by feasible transactions are less often discussed. This is possibly because economists usually look at aggregated data. For example, we may have access to an estimate of the sum of all wages earned by employees within a month, but we certainly do not have access to all of the individual payments made. Economic models have typically been developed to work with these aggregated variables, and the question of the underlying transactions is ignored.[6]

Another reason why economists look at aggregated transactions relates to how they historically visualised the economy. They focussed on barter transactions amongst individuals. The relative prices of goods being traded were adjusted–somehow–so that everyone maximises their evaluation of the trades (their "utility"). This adjustment took place before trades took place, and then the trades would take place simultaneously.

To give a simplified example, imagine a simple economy where people have differing amounts of coconuts and fish. They want to trade amongst themselves so that each person has a combination of coconuts and fish that best matches their desires.

The economists assumed that all trades had to be done on a "fair basis"; that is, all transactions had to occur with the same ratio of fishes to coconuts (for example, 2 coconuts = 1 fish). Additionally, they assumed that all participants would be allowed to trade at this price to the maximum of their desires ("the market clears").

The logic went:

- If the price of coconuts is too low (relative to fish), there would be more demand for coconuts than there would be a supply offered.
- If the price of coconuts was too high, there would more supply offered than there were would be demand.

Using the now-famous supply and demand curves, economists showed that the market would be balanced at some price, and everyone can go home satisfied. (To the extent people had goods to offer for trade; if you came to the market empty-handed, you would come home the same way.) The key is that all the trading takes place simultaneously "sometime."

The future was brought into the framework with the addition of for-

---

6   An exception would be agent-based models, which can model all the transactions within an economy. These models are new and somewhat unproven.

ward (or futures) transactions. (You can buy oil for delivery a year in the future now in the futures market.) However, the price adjustments are still just happening at a single point in time.

More recently, Dynamic Stochastic General Equilibrium (DSGE) models brought this framework closer to time series analysis by treating the economy as a sequence of such trading sessions. Each accounting period corresponds to one trading session.

Outside the mainstream, the notions of equilibrium and market clearing were rejected, but it was quite often the case that transactions were modelled as being essentially simultaneous during an accounting period (quarterly, monthly).

The reality is that transactions occur at highly granular points in time, and that these transactions are priced in a manner that does not depend upon the aggregate set of transactions within an accounting period. My assertion is that the pattern of possible transactions pins down the possible set of aggregated transactions within a period. That is, if a set of transactions would appear to make no sense individually, we cannot see an aggregate set of data that reflects such transactions.

In particular, this matters for government finance. You often hear the argument that the "bond vigilantes" can somehow discipline governments. Proponents of this and similar views will admit that they cannot name any examples of such discipline, but it *could* happen. My response is that it will not, as the underlying transactions they contemplate make little sense.

If all transactions within a month happened during one instant, it is easy to come up with stories in which all bond market participants move in the same direction. For example, "everybody" might want to sell, and with no buyers, the price of bonds would collapse.[7] In the case where trading occurs sporadically during the month, it is unclear why a bond holder would want to take large capital losses by attempting to sell large amounts quickly, as this might cause catastrophic underperformance versus other investors who leaned against the selling pressure. Even if you think something bad is going to happen to bond prices in the coming months, you want to exit your positions quietly, with the minimum of losses. I discuss this further in Section 6.6.

---

7   A falling price causes the yield on the bonds to go up. For those unfamiliar with bond pricing, a basic introduction is found in Appendix 1.

3.3 What Is a Central Bank?

Central banks are the object of controversy and discussion, particularly since the focus in macroeconomics has shifted almost exclusively to monetary policy. For my purposes here, I am not interested in discussing the central bank's role in stabilising the economy or inflation. Instead, all that I am currently concerned with is the role of a central bank as a bank.

The central banks in the developed countries have long histories, in some cases starting as private banks. If we ignore the issue of where they came from, modern central banks are banks that are typically characterised by the following:

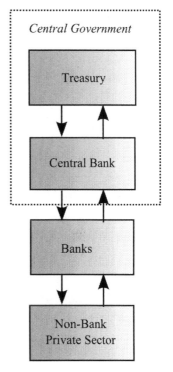

Central Government

Figure 3. *Monetary flows for central government*

1. they are owned by the central government;[8]
2. all of the other key banks within a banking system have a settlement account with the central bank;
3. the only non-bank clients of the central bank are the central government, and entities that are allowed to have accounts at the central bank by the government (such as foreign governments, for holding their currency reserves);[9]

---

8   Some central banks have minority private shareholders or shareholders at other levels of government. The ownership of the Federal Reserve System has become an object of controversy in some corners of the United States. This controversy is frankly ridiculous; the central government owns the common equity of the Federal Reserve System, and hence controls it; private banks need to buy preference shares (which offer no control) in exchange for being a "member of the club." This is just a disguised capital requirement, and if the Federal Reserve were less politically tone deaf, they would abolish it as an anachronism.

9   It is apparently still possible for some citizens to have a bank account at the Bank of England.

Figure 3 on page 17 illustrates the flow of monetary transactions, with the central bank acting as the key intermediary for the government. Throughout this description, I use the term "Treasury" to represent the fiscal side of the government, although this may be the "Ministry of Finance" in some countries, such as Canada.

The treasury has financial interactions with the rest of the economy via the issuance of government bonds and bills, and their associated payments (principal and interest). Even so, these interactions are mediated by primary dealers (definition[10])–which I lump in with the banks for simplicity herein–and the payment system.

In some cases, the central bank or the treasury will move government deposits from the central bank to private banks. This flow of deposits is used to smooth out liquidity needs within the banking system. This is one of the few times that the central government does not bank with the central bank. I discuss this further in Section 5.3.

The centralising role of the central bank means that the unit of account that it uses defines the unit of account within the wider domestic economy, as discussed in Section 2.2. For example, the Canadian dollar is effectively defined as one unit within the accounting system of the Bank of Canada.

I will not address the important area of the clearing system within my discussions. The central bank is a key player in ensuring that the clearing system operates without incident. Clearing is the process of transferring money between banks[11], and needs to be very carefully monitored. If you are receiving a billion-dollar transfer from another entity, you should be asking yourself very carefully whether that other entity actually has control of those billion dollars. However, since I am not concerned about discussing the risks within the private sector, I assume that payments will always clear without default. This allows us to ignore the role of the clearing system.

---

10   A primary dealer is a firm that has the right (and obligation) to directly bid at the auctions of Treasury Bonds and Bills. These can be banks, or specialist dealers (less common now).

11   In Canada, this is the Large Value Transfer System (LVTS). See "A Primer on Canada's Large Value Transfer System", by Neville Arjani and Darcey McVanel, Bank of Canada. URL: http://www.bankofcanada.ca/wp-content/uploads/2010/05/lvts_neville.pdf

Since the central bank is always the intermediary for the central government when dealing with other sectors of the economy, the study of monetary operations largely depends upon the operational framework of the central bank. The next sections lay out that framework.

3.4 Simplified Framework of Government Finance

The accounting and financial transactions of real world governments is a complex topic. However, in order to analyse a complex system, we have to make simplifications. I will now outline what I view is the simplest, yet realistic framework for government finance, which I will refer to as the Simplified Framework. Once we understand monetary operations within this framework, we can add new features to capture dynamics that were previously not modelled.

The model I am proposing is a cut down version of the framework that is currently being followed by the Federal Government of Canada. The United States model is quite different as the result of the use of bank reserves, discussed in Section 5.2. Other countries have removed mandatory reserves like Canada, but there can be small differences in procedures relative to the Simplified Framework.

The simplifications I add are not wholly unrealistic. One assumption is that private banks use government bonds and bills as "position-making instruments," which are instruments that are traded as a means of managing the liquidity positions of banks. Hyman Minsky traced the development of position-making instruments in the United States in Chapter 4 of *Stabilizing an Unstable Economy*. He observed that the main position-making instruments during the early post-World War II era were Treasury bills, which matches the assumption here.

The key simplification is that the notion of "reserves" has been abolished from the banking system. The only "money" used in Canadian government finance is currency—notes and coins—which have very limited impact upon the economy (other than the role that they play with regard to the zero lower bound for interest rates, as discussed in Section 4.2). This allows us to dispense with the discussions of the nature of money that tend to dominate other approaches to monetary economics. Nevertheless, once we understand this simplified "no reserves" model, we can bolt on reserves to see what they accomplish (in summary: very little). This is

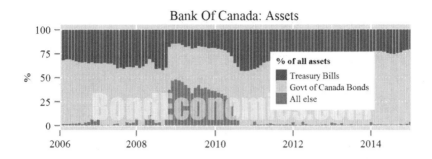

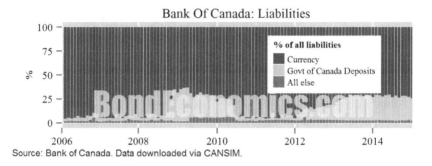

Source: Bank of Canada. Data downloaded via CANSIM.

Figure 4. *Bank of Canada balance sheet*

discussed in Chapter 5.

Within the Simplified Framework, the central bank balance sheet is described as follows.

1. Central bank assets only consist of government bonds and Treasury bills.

2. Central bank liabilities only consist of currency outstanding, and the central government deposit. Capital (or equity) is kept near zero by continuously paying out any profits as dividends to the central government.

In order for the central bank to keep this liability structure, private banks would have to ensure that their settlement balance at the central bank is always exactly zero at the end of the day.

Figure 4 shows the evolution of the assets and liabilities on the balance sheet for the Bank of Canada since 2006. The structure is close to the Simplified Framework (outside of the period around the Financial Crisis). There are some small deviations from the assumed structure; they are the small components we see at the bottom of the two panels. The Simplified Framework forces those deviations to be zero.

The Federal Government of Canada also follows one practice that I am ignoring for now–the Ministry of Finance lends money from its balance at the central bank to private banks in auctions. I discuss this in Section 5.3.

3.5 Consolidation of the Treasury and the Central Bank

One of the strengths of Modern Monetary Theory is that it provides a clean analytical framework for the analysis of economies with a free-floating currency. One of the ways in which it achieves this is to consolidate the central bank with the fiscal side of the central government. Such a consolidation has extremely important effects for understanding government default risk, and is controversial as a result. However, it should be noted that MMT does not rely solely upon simplifications; the MMT academic literature includes some detailed analysis of the legal institutions of governmental finance.[12]

Consolidation is a term from accounting, and it is a merger of the accounting statements of two (or more) entities. Financial analysts use consolidated accounting statements all of the time, possibly without realising it. Pretty well every major multinational "corporation" actually consists of dozens if not thousands of separate legal entities. When analysts look at the financial statements of a public corporation, what they are looking at are the consolidated statements of all of the underlying corporate entities.

What we are interested in here is the consolidation of the central bank and the rest of the central government, which is the "fiscal arm" of government–the Treasury (Ministry of Finance). For the purposes of economic analysis, we typically are only concerned with monetary policy and fiscal policy, and so we can ignore the other components of the central government (such as the judiciary).

An example of consolidation is given below, assuming the government follows my Simplified Framework.

---

12   Fullwiler, Scott T., Modern Monetary Theory - A Primer on the Operational Realities of the Monetary System (August 30, 2010). Available at SSRN: http://ssrn.com/abstract=1723198 or http://dx.doi. org/10.2139/ssrn.1723198

First is the balance sheet of the Treasury. I assume that the government has non-specified fixed assets with a value of $200, a deposit at the central bank, as well as 100% ownership of the central bank worth $5. The Treasury has $180 in bonds outstanding (which presumably includes Treasury bills as well). This leaves the government with capital (equity) of $55.[13]

Treasury

Assets		Liabilities	
Deposits at Central Bank	$30	Government Bonds	$180
Fixed Assets	$200		
Equity in Central Bank	$5	Capital	$55

The central bank does not have deposits from private banks ("reserves" or "settlement balances"). Therefore, the only liabilities of the central bank are currency (dollar bills and coins) as well as a deposit from the Treasury. The central bank operates with only $5 in capital, as central banks return profits to the Treasury as dividends rapidly. Since they are unable to go bankrupt, they do not need large capital cushions.

The central bank has only government bonds (including Treasury bills) as financial assets. This is the standard procedure for most "Anglo" countries; but it is not universal. The alternative is for the central bank to lend to private banks, so-called "overdraft economies" and is described in the Appendix 2.

Central Bank

Assets		Liabilities	
Government Bonds	$75	Currency	$42
Fixed Assets	$2	Deposit From Treasury	$30
		Capital	$5

What happens if we consolidate the central bank and the Treasury?

---

13   In my first online draft of this analysis, I had accounted for the Treasury as a stand-alone entity without including its equity stake in the central bank. I would like to thank Joseph Laliberté for spotting that problem.

When we consolidate two entities, we net out claims between the two. The result is:

Consolidated Government

Assets		Liabilities	
Fixed Assets	$202	Currency	$42
		Government Bonds	$105
		Capital	$55

The changes include:

- The central bank's holdings of government bonds are netted out. All we are left is the $105 in bonds that are held outside of the central bank.
- The Treasury's deposit at the central bank is both a liability and an asset to the consolidated entity, and is netted out to zero.
- Fixed assets represents all fixed assets on both balance sheets, and is the sum of the two values. The consolidated capital is equal to the original capital of the Treasury, as it already includes the capital of the central bank. (In a real world example, consolidated balance sheet valuations may be different than those for the unconsolidated entities. This might result from using historical costs versus market cost to value assets and liabilities. In such a case, capital would need to be adjusted to bring the balance sheet back into balance.)

From the perspective of entities outside the government, all that matters are their (net) financial assets, which are currency holdings ($42) and their government bond holdings ($105). These amounts are unaffected by consolidation. This is why consolidation makes for a cleaner economic model–it reduces the number of variables to be tracked, but it does not affect the position of the non-government sector.

Note that the real world accounting is much more complicated than my highly simplified example. However, the accounting used within an economic model need not slavishly follow accepted accounting principles, and so consolidation is easier within model economies. Since the objective here is creating mental models for the economy–rather than in producing documents that will need to be approved by an external auditor—I see little need to pursue such details. However, for those who are interested in such a treatment, the United Kingdom publishes a consolidated set of accounts—the *Whole of Government Accounts*.[14]

Finally, there is the question of why consolidation matters. Consolidating the central bank with the Treasury provides a much cleaner understanding of how the central government interacts with the other sectors of the economy. This appears entirely reasonable. However, there appear to be two broad reasons why the validity of consolidation is questioned.

1. There does not appear to be a reason why a central bank can default (in the absence of the external constraints that are the subject of Chapter 8). Consolidation with the Treasury implies that the Treasury is also default risk free, which would be objected to by those who are worried about a Treasury default.

2. By incorporating the central bank within the Treasury, the independence of monetary policy is questioned. Those who believe that the central bank ought to thwart the policy objectives of the Treasury might insist that the central bank be kept distinct.

I do not agree with either of those two stances, so I view consolidation as being valid. That said, these objections should be kept in mind if you use an analytical framework that relies upon consolidation.

3.6 Concluding Remarks

A key distinguishing feature between the central government and all other entities within the economy is that it owns the central bank. From the point of view of the private sector, it might as well treat the central bank as being consolidated with the rest of the government as an economic entity.

---

14 I would like to thank Neil Wilson, who publishes the "3spoken" blog *(www.3spoken.co.uk)* for pointing me to the consolidated accounts for the United Kingdom.

Chapter 4 Government Financial Operations

4.1 Introduction

Within the Simplified Framework for the central bank balance sheet described in the previous chapter the only assets that the central bank holds (at the end of the day, at least) are central government bonds and bills. Additionally, the central bank acts as the intermediary for the central government in its dealings with the private sector. This has an important implication: *all net transactions between the (consolidated) central government and the private sector have to be settled with a transfer of government bonds/bills (at the end of the day).* If other instruments were used to settle transactions, the central bank could end up with those instruments on its balance sheet, which is assumed not to happen within the Simplified Framework.

In other words, if the private sector needs to make a net payment to the central government at the end of the day, that payment is settled via the private sector transferring bonds/bills with that market value to the central bank.

Since there are multiple private banks, they can use whatever means to transfer settlement balances amongst themselves: interbank lending, repos, trading beaver pelts, whatever. The only constraint is that the sum of their balances with the central bank is $0 at the end of the day. (From the perspective of the government, it does not matter whether each bank has to have a $0 balance, or have a system where positive balances at some banks may be allowed to cancel out negative ones.)

The exception to the use of bills/bonds as settlement instruments is that currency (notes and coin) could be used in transactions. As I explain in the next section, this is normally not significant from the standpoint of government finances.

4.2 The Limited Role of Currency

It is common to associate "money" with stacks of notes (such as $100 bills). This shows up in the terms like "paper money" and "printing money." In practice, the bulk of transactions (in terms of value) utilise electronic transfers of money that consists of balances at banks

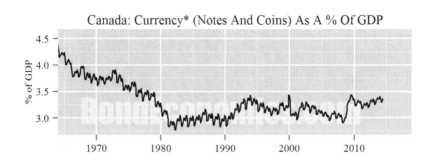

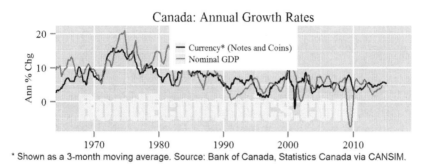

* Shown as a 3-month moving average. Source: Bank of Canada, Statistics Canada via CANSIM.

Figure 5. *Canadian currency outstanding*

(either a central bank or a private bank). The main exception is the underground economy (illegal transactions, or those done with cash to avoid taxes). Although the underground economy may be a significant area of activity, since it is non-taxed and largely non-measured, it is normally not of interest for an analysis of government finance. The underground economy only affects analysis in some cases, such as estimating the effect of a tax amnesty, or tighter enforcement of tax laws. Figure 5 illustrates the evolution of currency outstanding over time. Currency holdings decreased from over 4% of GDP in the 1960s to a value that has oscillated between 3% and 3.5% of GDP in recent decades. I have smoothed the currency series by averaging it over 3 months[15], as there are periodic spikes around December (reflecting higher holiday retail activity). Despite being smoothed in this fashion, the series still has a seasonal ripple.

The bottom panel shows the growth rates for nominal GDP (Gross Domestic Product including the effect of inflation) and cur-

---

15   Commonly referred to as a 3-month moving average.

rency growth. There is obviously a slight relationship (as the ratio of the two series is stable), but there is little direct correspondence in the growth rates on a year-to-year basis. This type of behaviour is termed a *stock-flow norm*, as it appears that households want to keep their *stock* of currency holdings stable relative to the *flow* of their nominal incomes, but it may drift around this target ratio in response to events.[16]

The operations involving currency are straightforward. Although it is possible for citizens to pay taxes with currency directly, this appears to be an unusual occurrence. Modern Monetary Theory authors enjoy pointing out that when this is done in the United States, the government gives the taxpayer a receipt and then destroys the bills received.[17] This also provides an example of Chartalist principles: money has value to the citizen in that it they can use it to remove a tax liability, but it has no real value to the issuing government.

Otherwise, transactions between the government and the banking sector involving cash revolve around the management of vault cash. Banks hold a certain amount of cash "in their vaults" and their automated teller machine network. Households typically withdraw currency from banks, which is then largely returned via retailers. Each private bank will have a circular flow of currency every day.

Eventually, banks need to restock their vaults. To do so, they will need to buy currency from the central bank (as Canadian and most other private banks cannot issue their own banknotes). Within my simplified system of governmental finance, the bank would first incur a drawdown in its settlement balance with the central bank, which would need to be settled by selling some government securities to the central bank by the end of the day

---

16   Since I am showing GDP, I am technically looking at all incomes within an economy, and not just households. I am following the usual convention of scaling economic aggregates by looking at their size relative to GDP.

17   For example, Warren Mosler observes in *Seven Deadly Innocent Frauds of Economic Policy*: "And what happens if you were to go to your local IRS office to pay your taxes with actual cash? First, you would hand over your pile of currency to the person on duty as payment. Next, he'd count it, give you a receipt, and hopefully, a thank you for helping to pay for social security, interest on the national debt, and the Iraq war. Then, after you, the tax payer, left the room, he'd take that hard-earned cash you just forked over and *throw it in a shredder*."

(assuming that the private bank did not have an inflow into its settlement balance from other transactions).

This means that we can visualise the transaction as a trade of government bonds/bills for currency.

Where does the central bank get the currency? It prints it (although it presumably has some stockpiles waiting in its vaults.) The newly printed money is a new liability for the Bank of Canada, matched by new assets–the bonds and bills it bought. (The balance sheet amounts have to match, as the market value of the bonds will equal the value of the currency purchased. These market values may bear limited resemblance to the face value of the bonds.)

Although I often see worries about governments "printing money," it is an extremely innocuous operation within this framework. It is an exchange of interest-bearing government bonds for currency–which pays no interest–at the behest of the private sector. The government's role is purely passive; it only "prints on demand."

The other side of this operation–private banks exchanging currency for bonds–is rarer as the stock of money follows an upward trend line, but it does happen when the demand for currency subsides in the new year.

These operations are generally of interest only for logistical purposes within the banking and retailing system. There is normally only a limited effect on government finances; the only effect is the amount of "seigneurage revenue," and that tends to be stable over time. (*Seigneurage* is the profit earned by the central bank by the fact that currency notes do not pay interest, while the central bank earns interest on its assets. More generally, the government earns a notional "profit" by replacing inter-paying debt with money. Seigneurage is also spelled "seigniorage" or even "seignorage.")

Currency possibly becomes more significant in its role in creating a lower bound for interest rates. Since notes hold their value over time, they are equivalent to a bank account that has an interest rate of 0%. This appears to rule out negative interest rates, as people can withdraw cash from banks rather than suffer from negative interest. (This lower limit for interest rates is often dubbed the zero lower bound, or ZLB.)

This used to be a topic of only academic interest until various European central banks set their policy rates to slightly negative levels. The open question is how much further they can lower interest rates until the private sector starts making large currency withdrawals, and stockpiling the cash.

My view is that these policies are crazy, and I hope that they will be abandoned soon. If negative rates are sustained, the technical details of how currency is handled could become quite important. Will it be possible for investors to withdraw large amounts of currency and store them safely? If this turns out to be infeasible, currency is not really an alternative for the entities that determine the pricing of government bonds. (There is an additional consideration that there are other mechanisms to achieve a 0% rate of return on investment, such as exercising your right to prepay taxes. These alternative means of insuring a 0% return on investment may prove to be a viable mechanism for the private sector to avoid negative interest rates.)

In summary, although negative interest rates are achievable, currency and other institutional factors will probably prevent interest rates from getting much more negative than -1% or so.

4.3 Transactions Not Involving Currency

There are a few basic types of operations within government finance that do not involve the use of currency. This section outlines how they affect governmental balance sheets. The types of operations are:

1. bond auctions;
2. tax payment;
3. government spending; and
4. principal repayment for government debt.

One principle to keep in mind is because the central bank is the intermediary in all transactions for the government, and that it only holds bonds and bills at the end of the day, all net transactions have to be "settled" via the transfer of bonds and bills between it and private sector banks. (Note that my use of "banks" here is a shortcut, as primary dealers are also counterparties of the central bank, and not all primary dealers are banks.) If we look at transactions in isolation, we can pretend that each transaction is settled via a bond/bill transfer, although the counterparties would only transact to cover the net flows of the day.

Bond Auctions. Periodically, the Treasury issues new bonds or bills in an auction. In Canada, the auction is conducted by the Bank of Canada on behalf of the Government of Canada (Ministry of Finance). Auction formats vary, but they typically involve the government setting the amount of bonds/bills to be auctioned, and the bidding from the private sector determines the price (yield). Appendix 1 discusses the price/yield relationship.

Normally, bond issuance is described as a means of "raising money." Once we realise that all transactions between the government and the private sector involve a transfer of bonds, one comes to an interesting problem: how can the private sector pay cash for new bonds when they are auctioned? The answer is that unless the private sector has previously run up a positive settlement balance that day at the central bank, it cannot–all it can do is exchange existing bonds for the new ones.

For example, the private sector could sell bonds that are near maturity to the central bank, in order to use the proceeds to buy the new longer-dated bonds. This is significant, as this increases the average maturity of bonds held by the private sector. If there were no new issuance, the bond market would disappear, as the average maturity drops by a day every day.

If we assume that the private sector did not have a previous positive settlement balance, issuing $100 in bonds will have the effect of

a) increasing the balance of the Treasury by $100 at the central bank,

b) putting $100 of new bonds in the hands of the private sector, which sells old bonds with a market value of $100 to the central bank, and

c) increasing the market value of bonds and bills held by the central bank. (Note that the Bank of Canada does tend to buy bonds at auction, and so a certain amount of the $100 would normally go straight to the Bank of Canada's balance sheet. This is unlike other countries, which have legal prohibitions against the central bank buying bonds at auction.)

Figure 6 shows the flows

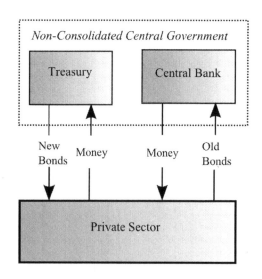

Figure 6. *Non-consolidated bond auction flows*

of money and bonds when we keep the Treasury separate from the central bank. The Treasury sells new bonds (for money), while the
central bank accepts old bonds in exchange for
money. (Money in this case means settlement
balances at the central bank.)

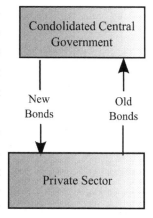

Figure 7 shows the situation when we consolidate the central bank with the Treasury.
The money flows cancel out, and all we are left
with is the exchange of old bonds for the new
bonds issued at auction. The interpretation of
these transactions is quite different, and gives
an example of the analytical advantage of consolidating the Treasury and the central bank
(Section 3.5).

Figure 7. *Consolidated bond auction flows*

What this means is that government debt auctions by themselves cannot raise the amount of government debt held by the private sector. Although the gross amount of central government debt rises, the market
value of debt held by the central bank will rise by the same amount. Since
the central government owns the central bank, this debt nets out if we
consolidate (and we ignore the accounting issue that the market value of
bonds bought may not match their face value).

Tax Payment. Tax payments typically are paid via cheque or a transfer
from the bank. If a taxpayer writes a cheque for $100 to the Treasury (in
Canada, the *Receiver General of Canada*), his chequing account at the bank
will be reduced by $100; that is, he has a smaller claim on the bank. In
order to settle the transaction, the bank needs to sell $100 of bonds/bills
to the central bank. The central bank also increases the Treasury's account
balance by $100.

In summary, a tax payment of $100 does the following:
   a)   reduces the market value of bonds held by the private sector by
        $100,
   b)   increases the market value of bonds held by the central bank by
        $100, and
   c)   increases the balance of the Treasury at the central bank by $100.

Spending/Principal Repayments. When the government spends, it issues a cheque to a recipient. (This also covers the other side of bond auctions, principal repayment.)

For example, the government sends a $100 cheque to a contractor. When the contractor deposits the cheque, the balance of her savings account at the bank is increased by $100; that is, she has a $100 larger claim on the bank. To match this increased liability, the central bank will transfer $100 to the bank's settlement account, and decrease the Treasury's balance by $100 (to keep the central bank's books balanced). If there were no other transactions that day, the central bank would have to sell $100 of bills or bonds to the private bank in order to bring the end of day settlement balances back to $0.

For the government, the effect is to:
  a) decrease the Treasury balance at the central bank by $100,
  b) decrease the market value of bills and bonds on the central bank's balance sheet by $100, and
  c) increase the market value of bonds held by the private sector by $100.

This illustrates a principle that is often discussed in MMT: government spending creates the income that allows the private sector to buy government bonds. *Government spending precedes borrowing.*

The only catch is that when the government spends, the Treasury balance decreases. What happens if it drops to nothing? (The other transactions–bond issuance and tax collection–increased the Treasury balance, and thus do not pose a problem on this front.)

4.4 Can the Treasury Run Out of Money?

The usual MMT response to the question "Can the Treasury run out of money?" is to explain that this is impossible. Although I agree with the MMT assessment, I would cautiously note that given sufficient human incompetence, many "impossible" things could be achieved. In the case of the Treasury running out of money, it would take some fairly heroic incompetence, but it might be achievable.

For example, at the time of writing, government deposits at the Bank of Canada are just over $22 billion (about 1% of GDP, although some amount of that is money held for other entities). If the Canadian Federal Government had the bright idea of mailing someone a $25 billion cheque, the balance of the Consolidated Revenue Fund would go negative, and the Bank of Canada may have the right to refuse to honour that cheque; that is, it would "bounce." (Please note that I have not looked into the legality of such a possibility, as I doubt that we would ever get to such a situation. I have seen opinions that the central bank would be forced to honour such cheques in some countries, but I am unaware of any such situation in practice.)

The first issue is that although governments do have rather large spending *programmes*, individual cheques of that magnitude are not written. Even if the federal government has a large military contract, payments are spread out over multiple years. Therefore, we do not see huge spikes in spending that could overwhelm the Treasury balance.

The second issue is that the Ministry of Finance owns the central bank, and can very easily grant itself the power to run an overdraft (a negative balance) at the Bank of Canada. Although the Bank of Canada is "independent," that "independence" only extends to the setting of interest rates and other aspects of monetary policy.

In any event, the Ministry of Finance is continuously watching the balance in the account, and monitoring all transactions. This is not just because of the fear of "running out of money" (which is a reasonable worry of a household); the Federal Government is a sprawling organisation, and care has to be taken that there are no irregularities. Even if the ability to run an open-ended overdraft were in place, good governance would require that the balance be watched like a hawk.

It is trivial to avoid a negative balance. All that needs to be done is keep a steady programme of debt issuance going, staying ahead of deficits, and maturing bonds. Moreover, if there is a sudden need to replenish the balance, it is easy to squeeze in an extra Treasury bill auction.

In order for a negative balance to occur, it would require either:

1. a poor forecast of net spending by the Ministry of Finance; or
2. an inability to raise its balance during bill and bond auctions ("rollover risk").

The first possibility revolves around incompetence, as I noted earlier. "Rollover risk" is more interesting and I will return to it in Section 6.6, once I have covered some preliminary concepts.

4.5 Concluding Remarks

What the central bank holds on its balance sheet dictates how private sector banks manage their liquidity. In a system where the central bank only owns government debt, the private sector has no choice but to use government bonds as position-making instruments. Other private sector entities can emit debts that can be used for liquidity purposes, but this usage is only provisional and can be withdrawn. A situation is created where government bonds have a privileged position *vis-à-vis* household and corporate debt. This creates a situation where the government needs to spend first, and then emit debt later. The government does not need the private sector to lend it money, since "money" is just another liability of government. Bond issuance just allows the private sector to rearrange its holdings of government liabilities.

Chapter 5 Extensions–Reserves, Government Lending

5.1 Introduction

This chapter covers two additional complexities contained in real world economies. The most important extension to the framework is the addition of bank reserves, which are still a feature of the regulation of banking in the United States. The second is lending by the Treasury (Ministry of Finance).

5.2 Bank Reserves

Bank reserves are deposits by private banks at the central bank. They were abolished in Canada and elsewhere, but they still exist in the United States. Within conventional approaches to economics, reserves are viewed as extremely important, particularly as the standard textbooks are mainly written by Americans.

Please note that this usage of the word "reserves" is different from its use with respect to the concept of *loan loss reserves,* which is a synonym for loan loss provisions. Businesses (particularly banks) make a loan loss reserve when they write down the estimated value of debts that they are owed because the loans are seen as non-collectable. Although bank reserves have been abolished in Canada, this does not mean that they no longer have to hold reserves against prospective credit losses.

Although other financial institutions have bank-like characteristics, banks operate in a distinctive manner. This is because banks have special legal privileges. For example, one can pay off debts by a transfer of a bank deposit (cheques, electronic transfer), whereas other means of payment can be rejected by lenders. These special privileges make some people angry[18], as it puts banks in an advantageous position versus competitors. However, the cost of those privileges is that banks face a relatively strict regulatory environment.

Other financial institutions largely only exist as a means of bypass-

18   Evidence for this is easily found within internet discussions. For example, a search for the phrase "fractional reserve banking is the root of our problems" produced over 92,000 results at the time of writing.

ing the regulatory regime banks face. For example, money market funds
take over the deposit-taking function of the banking system, while facing negligible capital requirements. Services can be offered cheaper, as
the capital and regulatory compliance costs are lower. (The Financial Crisis emanated from the largely non-regulated "shadow banking system,"
which shows that there are costs borne by others–dubbed *externalities* in
economics jargon–created by these cheaper services. Banks were generally dragged into the crisis by their non-bank financial subsidiaries.)

Reserves are one means of regulating the banking system. The
principles behind them are straightforward, although the details are
complex (as banks continuously find ways to work around the regulations). Reserves are supposed to create a liquidity buffer sup-
porting bank demand deposits–deposits that customers can pull
out of the bank immediately (either via cheque or withdrawal).

At the end of a *reserve maintenance* period (every two weeks in the case
of the United States), the amount of "demand deposits" at the bank is calculated. (Whether a particular deposit at a bank is considered a "demand
deposit" is defined by regulations.) This amount is then multiplied by the
reserve ratio, such as 10%, to get the amount of required reserves. (For
example, if a small bank had $100 in demand deposits, and the reserve
ratio is 10%, it would have to hold $10 in reserves.) This is the amount of
reserves that will be needed to be held during the next accounting period.[19]

Reserves are deposits held at the central bank (in the United States,
the Federal Reserve System). I described these "settlement balances" earlier. The difference from the "simplified model" I describe and a model
with reserves is that the target settlement balance at the end of the day
is no longer zero–it is the level of regulatory reserves. Note that banks
are allowed to have a settlement balance that is greater than the required
reserves (termed "excess reserves"), but not a lesser amount. To make
up a deficiency, banks are forced to borrow at the Fed's Discount Win-

---

19   The fact that the required reserves are based on the previous period's
deposits is not a minor technicality from the standpoint of theory. It means
that the conventional description of how bank reserves operate is incorrect.
Since the required reserves are essentially fixed during a time period, banks
have no means of reducing its required reserves by calling in loans if there
is an insufficient aggregate amount of reserves within the banking system.

dow, and regulators will start asking the bank management team very awkward questions about the bank's operations. Meanwhile, other private sector entities might question the creditworthiness of a bank that is continuously forced to go to the central bank for funding. (This stigma does not apply to "overdraft economies," as discussed in Appendix 2.)

If we look at how the banking system in the United States operated before the financial crisis, the banking system held only a minimal amount of excess reserves. Typically, banks with excess reserves would trade them away to those with deficiencies in the fed funds market. (In Minsky's terminology, fed funds are a position-making instrument.) It would be safe to approximate the amount of excess reserves with zero within a model.

(The situation changed after the Federal Reserve instituted quantitative easing. The Federal Reserve bought bonds, which injected money into the banks' reserve positions. This is the subject of Section 5.4.)

However, if we look at our Simplified Framework, we see that the addition of reserves actually makes very little difference. Under the assumption that excess reserves are zero at the end of the day, the aggregate required reserves will be a fixed amount within an accounting period. All the net flows I previously described would work in exactly the same way, as bill/bond holdings would have to be adjusted to hit this fixed reserve target, rather than zero.

We can think of required reserves as being a special government bond, issued by the central bank, which has an overnight maturity. Since required reserves normally do not pay interest, this means that banks are stuck with bonds that pay 0% interest. One could interpret this as a means of "financial repression," a sneaky way for the government to reduce its interest costs by forcing the financial sector to lend to it at "below market" rates.

Many countries, including Canada, decided that this was a bad idea. Since banks make sure that they are profitable, customers effectively pay the "reserves tax" as the result of banks adjusting net interest margins in the banks' favour. (The *net interest margin* is the spread between the interest rate at which the bank lends to customers versus what it pays on deposits.) This forced increase in banks' required net lending margin disadvantages banks versus the rest of the financial system (which happens to be less regulated).

It should be noted that eliminating reserves does not mean that banks are unconstrained in their ability to create loans. (This is a prediction of the "money multiplier" that is found in undergraduate economics textbooks.) Banks need to hold capital (equity and various forms of "pseudo-equity," such as preferred shares and subordinated debt) against their assets. The riskier the assets, the more capital that needs to be held against them. The Basel international regulatory framework for banks sets out such rules, although the implementation varies from country to country. For the purposes of the report, the key feature of bank capital regulation is that (central) government bonds typically do not require capital to be held against them ("0% risk weighting").

To summarise, the addition of reserves makes very little difference to my simplified model, other than changing the level of settlement balance target. This does not change end-of-day settlement behaviour in a significant fashion.

5.3 Government Lending

The simplified model I present might appear too simplistic. It ignores one important class of operations, which consists of government short-term lending to the banking system. This typically takes one of the following forms:

1. the central bank "lends" to private sector counterparties (banks and primary dealers) via repurchase agreements ("repos," which are described below); and
2. the Treasury lends to the private banks.

There exists a third category of lending, which is where the central bank lends money (settlement balances) to private banks that put up private sector assets as collateral. This is frequently done in "overdraft" economies (Appendix 2), but within the types of monetary systems that I am discussing here, this is only used in emergencies.

A repo is an agreement between two parties that resembles a form of lending against collateral. However, the collateral is transferred outright. The "borrower" sells a bond at a fixed price to the "lender." The lender owns the bond, until the expiry of the repo transaction, at which point the bond is sold back to the original owner (the "borrower"). The price at which the bond is sold back is usually higher, and the increase in price acts as an implicit form of interest payment.[20] The implicit interest rate is the *repo rate*, which is how the terms are quoted in the market. Repo

---

20   If there is an intervening coupon payment, the payment is adjusted to take this into account.

transactions are generally very short term (such as overnight), but they can be extended to longer maturities (typically under a year) in *term repos*. The "lender" is in a very secure position.

1. The original seller is obligated to buy back the bond at the agreed price, regardless of the status of the bond. Therefore, the seller provides the first line of defense for repayment.

2. If the seller is unable to buy back the bond (typically as the result of bankruptcy), the "lender" is guaranteed repayment by the issuer of the bond. The market value of the bonds is larger than the amount "lent" (the reduction in the amount lent is known as a "haircut"), so the "loan" is more than covered.

This double layer of credit protection makes repos attractive to money market investors. This means that repos are used both by the formal banking system, as well as by the non-bank financial sector.

For holders of government bonds, repos have advantages over selling the bonds to raise cash. If the need for cash is temporary, there is no risk of having to buy back the bonds at a higher price (lower yield). This allows banks to adjust their liquidity positions without disturbing their bond portfolios. Additionally, the yield of bonds is typically higher than the repo rate ("positive carry"), and so "borrowing" against them tends to be profitable.

The fact that repo transactions are attractive to the private sector provides one incentive for the central bank to adjust the net settlement balances of banks by using repos. Additionally, if the central bank holds repos as assets, the size of the repo positions can be run down without having to sell bonds. As long as bonds are never sold outright, the central bank can avoid losses (as their bond holdings are typically not marked-to-market on their balance sheet). This means that they will not run into negative capital (equity) when they raise interest rates. A negative capital position for a central bank is not an economic issue (it cannot go bankrupt), but it could be embarrassing politically.

Before 2008, repos were a large portion of the assets held by the U.S. Federal Reserve. (Since then, outright bond purchases under the "Quantitative Easing" program pushed the balance sheet towards outright bond holdings.) The Bank of Canada, however, generally does not have very large repo positions (although they are used occasionally), as shown by the small percentage of non-government bond assets on their balance sheet.[21]

Lending by the Treasury is another tool used to deal with settlement imbalances. In some countries, the central bank may move Treasury deposits to private banks to inject cash into the private sector. This is effectively a loan from the Treasury to the private sector. This was extensively done in the United States before the advent of the Federal Reserve Bank system.

In Canada, the Ministry of Finance has an explicit programme of lending from the Consolidated Revenue Fund (its account at the central bank).

These different methods of lending money to private banks has the consequence that it is possible to transfer cash to the private sector from the government, without requiring the private sector sell bonds to the central bank (as was the previous assumption). Bond auctions create a large need for settlement balances within the private sector, as the winners of the auction need to pay for the bonds. In order to avoid disruption in the markets, the government increases those settlement balances before the auction via repos or direct lending from the Treasury. When the bidders pay for the bonds, the settlement balances return to the government. *In summary: the government lends the private sector the settlement balances needed to pay for the bonds it auctions.* In other words, auctions are not a means of raising money for the consolidated central government.

The fact that the private sector needs to borrow money from the central government in order to allow it to buy government bonds is one of the more counter-intuitive insights of Modern Monetary Theory. For example, Warren Mosler described the process in the United States within his book, *Seven Deadly Innocent Frauds of Economy Policy.*

> *For those of you who understand reserve accounting, note that the Fed can't do what's called a reserve drain without doing a reserve add. So what does the Fed do on settlement day when Treasury balances increase? It does repos—to add the funds to the banking system that banks then have to buy the Treasury securities. Otherwise, the funds wouldn't be there to buy the Treasury securities, and the banks would have overdrafts in their reserve accounts. And what are overdrafts at the Fed? Functionally, an overdraft is a*

---

21   I was concerned that I was missing something in the accounting treatment for repos used by the Bank of Canada. A spokesperson confirmed by email that there was no re-categorisation of repos into other categories.

loan from the government. Ergo, one way or another, the funds used to buy the Treasury securities come from the government itself. Because the funds to pay taxes or buy securities come from government spending, the government is best thought of as spending first, and then collecting taxes or borrowing later.[22]

5.4 Aside: Quantitative Easing

Quantitative Easing (QE) is a rather silly central bank practice that became popular after the Financial Crisis. It had previously been adopted by the Bank of Japan during its battle with the mild Japanese deflation, but then it was undertaken by the United States Federal Reserve, which was desperate to remain relevant after it had lowered its policy rate to zero.

Quantitative Easing is the practice of the central bank purchasing government bonds from the private sector in order to grow the size of its balance sheet. Within a monetary system that uses bank reserves (such as the United States), these purchases create excess reserves within the banking system. (In my Simplified Framework, such a policy could not be implemented, as settlement balances are assumed to remain at zero.)

This is supposed to affect the economy as the result of two mechanisms.

1. **Quantity Theory of Money.** Since bank reserves are considered part of the monetary base, this policy would be considered inflationary by those who believe in the Quantity Theory of Money. They will act on those expectations, and use money to buy goods and services that they believe will rise in price.

2. **Supply effects.** By reducing the amount of bonds outstanding, the average maturity of government debt falls, and this reduction in the supply will raise the price of bonds (which lowers long-term interest rates). Lowering long-term rates makes borrowing more attractive, which allegedly will boost economic growth.

The first mechanism–the Quantity Theory of Money–is frankly disreputable. In its simplest form, the theory says that if we double the amount of money in an economy, and hold all else equal, the price level will double. This theory has a long history within economics, and there are many within the financial markets who strongly believe in it. Central bank economists supposedly did not believe in it,

---

22   Footnote 2 on page 20 of the 2010 edition of *Seven Deadly Innocent Frauds of Economic Policy.*

but they were happy to prey upon the gullibility of the believers.

The Quantity Theory of Money is generally hard to disprove empirically. If you refer back to the chart in Section 4.2, the amount of currency in circulation in Canada has been stable as a percentage of nominal GDP. (Since there are no longer reserves in Canada, the amount of currency outstanding largely represents the "monetary base.") In other words, there does appear to be a multiplier between money and the size of the economy in nominal terms, and if the economy grows faster due to inflation, the amount of currency would be expected to rise.

The problem with the Quantity Theory of Money is that the stock of money cannot be controlled by the central bank to determine the price level. For example, if the economy is growing slowly (in nominal terms), is it possible to speed it up by increasing the growth rate of money? This was a core idea behind Monetarism, and central banks discovered that they were unable to control the money supply in a useful fashion. It is easy to see the problem with the theory within the Simplified Framework. The money supply consists of currency in circulation. If my income is rising in dollar terms as well as the dollar prices of goods, it is reasonable to assume that I will hold more cash in my wallet. However, there is no mechanism by which the Governor of the Bank of Canada can induce me to withdraw cash from my bank account. In other words, the money supply cannot be used as a variable to control the economy.

The second mechanism—the reduction of supply—appears more plausible. I am somewhat of a fundamentalist in my belief that expectations determine bond yields (as discussed in Appendix 3), but I am willing to concede that a large enough binge of buying by the central bank can lower bond yields. The Bank of Japan engineered such a squeeze in the markets in 2014-2015. That said, the effect does not appear to be significant relative to the variability of rate expectations. Quantitative Easing was effective more as a signalling device: if the Fed is buying bonds, that is a sign that they will not hike rates any time soon. This drops yields by lowering the expected path of short-term rates.

Measuring the effectiveness of the reduction of supply is also bedeviled by the issue that the central bank purchases are not the only thing that affects the maturity structure of government debt. The Treasury can modify the weighted average of debt outstanding by changing its issuance patterns. Yet I have never seen a convincing study that relates the weighted average maturity of government debt to bond yields.

There was a wave of studies by economists in the private sector and central banks "proving" that the Fed's Quantitative Easing policies lowered bond yields by very specific amounts. However, none of the articles that I read controlled for the pattern of issuance by the Treasury. And guess what? The Treasury lengthened the maturity of the debt it auctioned, largely cancelling out the effect of Fed purchases. Ignoring this effect is particularly embarrassing, as the consensus was that a similar policy–"Operation Twist," undertaken in the 1960s–failed precisely because the Treasury lengthened the maturity of the debt it auctioned.[23]

5.5 Concluding Remarks

Bank reserves are given too much prominence within discussions of the monetary system. They are just a form of government liabilities that are forced upon the banking system by regulators. They create a disadvantage for banks versus less regulated financial institutions, which is counterproductive.

The fact that governments lend to the private sector adds to the complexity of the financial system, but it is not strictly necessary. It just provides a means to smooth the effects of government cash flows–notably bond auctions–without forcing the banking sector to trade bonds and bills. Interestingly enough, it shows that bond auctions are not really a means for the government to "raise money," as the government is actually lending the money to the private sector in order to allow it to bid at the auctions.

---

23   For a discussion, see the box "Operation Twist Revisited" on page 45 of the BIS Quarterly Review, June 2009. URL: http://www.bis.org/publ/qtrpdf/r_qt0906.pdf

Chapter 6 Bonds and Interest Rates

6.1 Introduction

This report has so far ignored government interest payments, which is the primary reason why many people are interested in government finance. Although bond yields are determined within markets, the government–via the central bank–has the ability to set approximate limits for bond yield movements. This is quite unlike the situation for other borrowers, whose interest costs are largely outside of their control.

Within this chapter, the text assumes that the reader has some familiarity with how government debt securities–bills and bonds–are priced (that is, the relationship between prices and yields). Appendix 1 contains some background information for those who are less familiar with bond pricing.

6.2 Bond Yields and the Debt-to-GDP Ratio

The notion of supply and demand appears to cause the most difficulty for analysts and investors in the bond market. Supply and demand curves are one of the few things that most people remember from their economics courses, and they feel that it makes sense that this idea can be applied to the government bond market.

This shows up in discussions of the debt-to-GDP ratio.[24] The argument is that as the amount of debt outstanding relative to national income rises, the increasing supply of bonds will lower bond prices. (The implication is that bond yields would rise, as bond yields and prices move inversely.)

Figure 8 on page 46 shows the annual average of Treasury 10-year bond

---

24   Some people dislike the debt-to-GDP ratio, as it is the ratio of a stock (debt outstanding) to a flow (GDP). I do not feel that this is a problem, as we typically scale quantities by GDP to make comparisons easier. However, because of this mismatch in types of variables, there is no reason that any level of the debt-to-GDP ratio has any special significance. Therefore, the mystical properties that people attach to the 100% debt-to-GDP ratio is a mistake, which was costly for those who used such reasoning to short the Japanese Government Bond market.

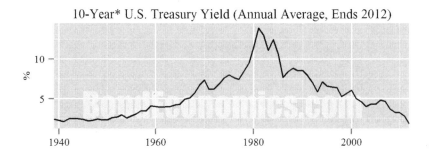

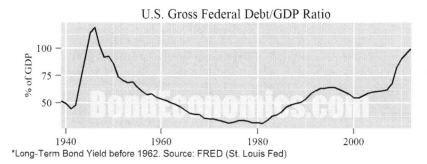

*Long-Term Bond Yield before 1962. Source: FRED (St. Louis Fed)

Figure 8. *U.S. Treasury Yield and the debt/GDP ratio*

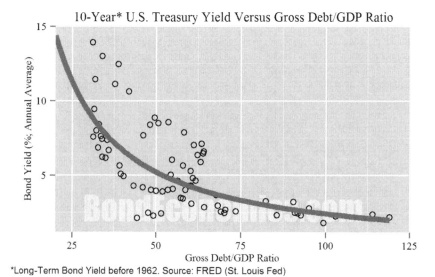

*Long-Term Bond Yield before 1962. Source: FRED (St. Louis Fed)

Figure 9. *Scatter plot of Treasury yield versus the debt-to-GDP ratio*

yields, and the Federal gross debt-to-GDP ratio. (Before 1962, "long-term" Treasury yields are used instead of the constant-maturity 10-year bond.)

When we look at a scatter diagram of bond yields versus the debt/GDP ratio, the relationship does not meet intuitive expectations. A basic fitting of the data[25] shows that increased debt/GDP ratios are associated with lower bond yields (Figure 9).

The Japanese Government Bond (JGB) market offers the best exam-

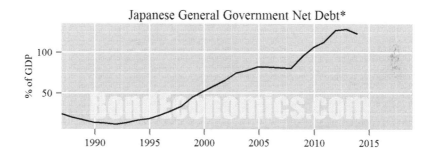

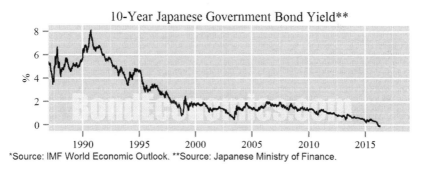

*Source: IMF World Economic Outlook. **Source: Japanese Ministry of Finance.

Figure 10. *Japanese debt-to-GDP ratio and bond yield*

---

25   I regressed the logarithm of the yield on the logarithm of the debt/GDP ratio. This is the easiest way to get a fitting of the obviously nonlinear relationship in the scatter diagram. (A linear regression will have problems fitting the data.) It should be noted that I have no theoretical reason why logarithms should be used. To have a more satisfying result, we would need to create a model, and then fit the model predictions to observed data. Unfortunately, the form of such a model would be controversial, and so I use just a basic statistical fit.

ple of the weakness of the effect of the debt-to-GDP ratio on yields. Figure 10 on page 47 shows the debt-to-GDP ratio for Japan, as well as the (nominal) 10-year JGB yield. Many investors have argued that the low yields on JGBs are "unsustainable," and they have ended up losing money positioning for higher bond yields. (This has become infamous, and the short-JGB trade is now referred to as "the Widowmaker Trade.")

These data provide reasons why I believe that simplistic theories that suggest that increasing the debt-to-GDP ratio will have a measurable increase in bond yields have to be rejected. It may be possible to find more complex theories in which high debt-to-GDP ratios will raise bond yields "someday." However, the analysis of such theories would presumably require addressing concepts that are beyond the scope of this report. (I am unaware of any theory of this type that is convincing, but others might disagree with that assessment.)

6.3 Marginal Analysis and Bond Yields

An alternative means of discussing supply and demand effects in the bond market is to look at "transactions at the margin." That is, look at the effect of one policy change in isolation, and see how it affects the economy. In this case, we want to see what happens if the government increases spending by a relatively small amount, and then see how this increased spending is supposed to affect bond yields–"all else equal."

A simple version of such an argument is as follows. Assume that the government wants to spend $100 million dollars on a new bridge.

Within "classical economics," the usual description of the operations is as follows.

1. The government needs to raise $100 million so its cheque will not bounce. It issues a $100 million bond.
2. The bond issuance creates new supply, and so bond yields will need to rise so that investors will be willing to hold the new bond in their portfolios.
3. The government uses the auction proceeds to redeem the $100 million cheque.

In summary, the new spending raises bond yields as the result of supply and demand.

The MMT riposte is to argue that the actual sequence of events is like this (for countries that use reserves).

1. The government issues a cheque, which is cashed.
2. This creates excess reserves in the banking system, which *lowers* interbank reserve lending rates.
3. The government needs to issue $100 million in bonds to mop up the excess reserves, returning interest rates back to where the central bank desires them to be.

I have my doubts about this style of analysis. In the Simplified Framework I use here, the treasury is always starting with a positive balance in its account at the central bank, and it can always meet a marginal payment like this by drawing down its balance slightly. Eventually, it may need to ramp up its bond issuance programme to replenish its account balance, but that could happen a few years in the future. Since there is a continuous cycle of spending and bond issuance, there is no way to determine which is "first," and therefore determine which story is correct.

Turning to a less theoretical discussion, there is considerable interest in the fixed income markets about the effect of auctions on yields. There appears to be a pattern of yields rising ahead of bond auctions, and then dipping back thereafter. It is very difficult to isolate this effect from other factors that move interest rates, but there is enough of a pattern that some investors can make money trading it over time. However, it must be underlined that this is a temporary effect; interest rates are not permanently increased by the auction. (If it were a permanent effect, bond yields would be continuously rising.) The only implication of this for government finance is that the yields paid on auction days are slightly elevated to the average of secondary market yields on either side of the auction. This has the effect of a slight increase of borrowing costs, and a boost to the profits of primary dealers who are purchasing at auction (which gives a hint as to why this effect occurs).

If there is a larger increase in the government deficit (the announcement of either a new spending programme or a tax cut), bond yields *should* rise. This is the result of the stimulative effect of this change in fiscal policy: nominal GDP growth would be higher because of this policy change, and that implies somewhat higher inflation as well. This should cause the central bank to react (as described in the following sections). I see no reasonable way of separating an "increased supply raises bond yields" effect from a "growth raising bond yields" effect. The only way of separating them is to create an extremely accurate bond yield model, and then we can use it to determine the exact breakdown of the factors driving bond yields. Unfortunately, the creation of such a model is the Holy Grail of fixed income analysts, and there is little sign that anyone has succeeded in doing so.

6.4 Central Bank Control of Short Rates

One of the distinguishing characteristics of interest rates relative to other financial markets is that short-term interest rates are administered by the central bank. The only other financial assets whose price is sometimes administered are currencies within currency peg arrangements (Chapter 8).[26]

The administrative determination of short-term rates is a cause for distress for some market fundamentalists, but this is a misunderstanding. The base rate of interest a bank will pay on its deposits, or what it charges to lend, is under the control of bank officers. A private bank needs to keep in mind its cost of capital when setting interest rates, but in the case of the central bank, its costs of capital is 0% (the rate of interest on currency). The central bank is the monopoly supplier of settlement balances, and it has the power to set unilaterally the cost required to borrow them. If the central bank did not administer the rate, what would it do—ask its bank counterparties what they think would be fair? Any private bank that ran its business on such a foolish premise would be very rapidly driven out of business.

Technically, most central banks only set the interest rate for deposits held "overnight" (one working day, which can be a few nights on a long weekend). One could then argue that any longer maturity can then be determined "in the market." This does not take into account how central banks operate. They do not announce an overnight rate every working day (although they might during a crisis). Instead, the rates committee only meets periodically. In Canada and the United States, there are usually eight rate setting meetings during a year, so there is typically a six-week period in between meetings.

---

26   Studies by post-Keynesian economists show that most prices within the real economy (that is, the nonfinancial economy) are also quite often administered without respect to near-term supply and demand pressures.

The implication is that the central bank is going to have to influence interest rates for terms longer than overnight. For example, imagine that the central bank is trading 2-week instruments (bills, repos) with banks 6 weeks ahead of the next meeting. It would be utterly unacceptable to the central bank to trade those instruments at a rate of 2% if the overnight target rate over the next 6 weeks is supposed to be 1%. It would be expected to lean against such a pricing by pushing 2-week yields lower. Given that the central bank has unlimited capacity to buy any instrument that it is eligible to purchase, its counterparties would have no real choice but to toe the central bank's line.

Central banks do not apply excessive efforts to keep such rates exactly on target, as there are various technical issues that can cause short-term rates to jump around. That said, deviations of hundreds of basis points (one basis point is 0.01%) are unacceptable, and we do not see them in practice. Therefore, we can think of short-term rates as being administered by a committee at the central bank, although we have to accept that there are small deviations around the policy rate.

6.5 Rate Expectations and the Term Premium

There is not a great deal of debate over the fact that central banks are able to pin down very short-term interest rates with limited chance of those rates departing from their targets. (With the understanding that particular types of short-term instruments can diverge for technical reasons.) However, this control appears to break down for "longer-term" instruments, whose interest rates are set by market participants. Precisely where the line is between "short-term" and "longer-tem" may depend upon whom you are talking to. (Central bankers sometimes refer to 3-year bonds as "long-term," a designation that might raise eyebrows amongst traders who deal in swaps from 20- to 50-year maturities.)

My view is that central banks have considerable *indirect* control over yields going out to 10 years in maturity or so, after which various "technical factors"[27] take over. My argument revolves around the entirely convention-

---

27   The term "technical factors" is a shorthand expression used by bond market strategists. Examples include the effect of regulations, taxes, or the demand for fixed income assets to match liabilities. Not every strategist will agree as to which factors matter, but they will agree that these factors exist.

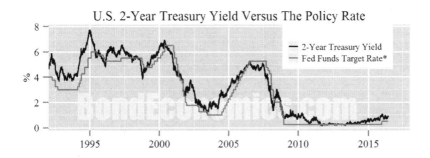

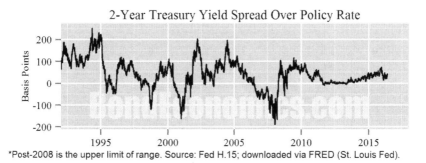

*Post-2008 is the upper limit of range. Source: Fed H.15; downloaded via FRED (St. Louis Fed).

Figure 11. *2-year U.S. Treasury yield and the policy rate*

al rate expectations view of bond yield determination. (For example, mainstream Dynamic Stochastic General Equilibrium models typically have an extremely fundamentalist version of rate expectations built into them.) Bond prices are somewhat erratic–like other financial market prices–so there are some nuances to my views. My argument is that the best way to understand interest rates is to start with a fundamentalist rate expectations view, and then add in complicating factors.

Since this is not a primer on how to trade bonds, I will not pursue those complications. Additionally, the topic inherently requires more mathematics than I wish to use within this report. As I believe that the mathematics is secondary in importance, I have deferred the details to Appendix 3. To summarise the key result of that Appendix: with a pure rate expectations explanation of interest rates, the yield on a bond is equal to the average of the short-term rate (which is set by the central bank) over the lifetime of the bond.

If there is a term premium, the bond yield will be slightly higher. That is,

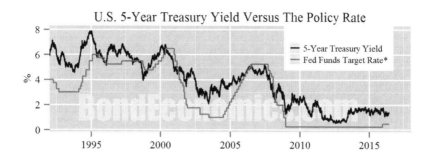

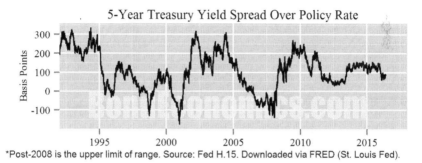

*Post-2008 is the upper limit of range. Source: Fed H.15. Downloaded via FRED (St. Louis Fed).

Figure 12. *5-year U.S. Treasury yield and the policy rate*

since buying a bond is riskier than holding "cash," it yields slightly more than what you expect from holding "cash" over the lifetime of the bond. (Cash in bond market parlance is extremely short maturity instruments that pay a rate near the policy rate of the central bank.)

Arguably, it is very difficult to forecast what the central bank will do over the next 30 years, but we have a better idea of what will happen over 2 or even 5 years.

Figure 11 on page 52 demonstrate that the data are consistent with this view. In the United States, the 2-year bond yield tracks the Fed's policy rate closely. Most of the time it is within 100 basis points (1%) of the policy rate. The deviations correspond to what the market expects the central bank to do over the coming 2 years.

Figure 12 shows that the spread of the 5-year bond yield over the policy rate can be greater, even hitting 300 basis points. This is what one would expect, as there is considerable scope for short rates to change over 5 years. That said, the yield is in the same ballpark as the policy rate; it is not thousands of basis points higher.

The implication of rate expectations theory is that this behaviour will continue. If this is the case, it will always be possible for the government to issue debt at levels near the policy rate (for shorter maturities, at least). This implies that the Treasury will always be able to replenish its balance at the central bank. The next section discusses whether this mechanism can break down.

6.6 Rollover Risk

In this section, we are looking at the possibility of involuntary default by a central government that is the result of being unable to raise the Treasury balance by issuing new debt. The most likely trigger of such a scenario is the need to issue new debt to replace maturing debt. This replacement is called "rolling over the debt," and so the risk of such a default is usually termed "rollover risk" by bond market analysts.

To summarise my views, I do not see such an event as being a serious possibility. There is no way "the markets" can force a government that finances itself in a manner similar to the Simplified Framework to default. (As I discuss in Chapter 8, governments that fix their currency parity or borrow in a foreign currency routinely default; this chapter applies to governments without such constraints.)

That said, it is not safe to say that such a sovereign *cannot* default. There are some obvious non-financial reasons why a government might default on its debt, and the most relevant historically is that the country has lost a war and the government no longer exists. Otherwise, the possibilities are voluntary decisions by the government (although it may be that the alternatives appear worse). *The key is that the decision to stop bond payments is taken by the government, and not the bond markets.* Examples of such voluntary reasons to default are given below.

- Radicals could be elected upon a platform of defaulting on the government debt as a means of reducing the wealth of the rich.
- As I noted earlier, given enough incompetence, the Treasury could find itself in a position where it has a negative balance at the central bank. (I view government incompetence as being a voluntary decision; others may not agree with that assessment.)
- Legal procedures associated with government finance could trig-

ger a default. The most notorious example is the debt ceiling in the United States. If it is not raised, it could force the Federal Government to default on debt payments. (There is a variety of untested legal opinions about what courses of action the Treasury must take in this case.)

- The size of interest costs could grow so large (or inflation so high) that the government will have no palatable alternative but to default on its debt. I am not hugely impressed with many of the arguments about financial constraints facing governments, but this is one of the few that I see as being at least plausible. That said, I do not think such an event is likely, for reasons that are briefly introduced in Section 7.7.

The main reason why a government does not face involuntary default risk is that the central bank effectively sets the interest rate on its short-term debt. A purist would argue that this is not exactly true, but the reality is that short-term rates are relatively close to where administered policy rates are (as illustrated in Section 6.5). Moreover, the central bank is a large player in the government bond market. (At least outside of "overdraft economies"; see Appendix 2.) Since the central bank has unlimited capacity to buy bonds, it can pin short-term bill prices pretty much wherever it wants. Then all the Treasury needs to do to increase its settlement balance is to issue short-term debt, which will be close to where the central bank is setting short-term rates.

This mechanism would break down under a decision of voluntary default. If the government announced a policy of defaulting upon its debts in two weeks, bond and bill prices would drop to whatever level market participants feel the salvage value of the debt would be, and the central bank would have an extremely difficult time trying to prop up bill prices (other than buying all of the debt offered to it). The question then arises: Can the private sector create such a situation without the trigger of a default announcement? The argument here is that it cannot.

The main problem with the theory that the private sector can suddenly reject ownership of government debt is that it requires everyone to move in the same direction simultaneously. An announcement of a default by an issuer creates an obvious catalyst for such an event. Otherwise, what would trigger such a reaction?

If one investor decided to get out of government debt, it has to do something with the proceeds, and simultaneously, the new buyer has to pay somehow for the bonds. The only way this can occur is that there is a circular exchange of financial assets amongst a number of investors (where I include "cash balances" or "money" as financial assets). We can divide the private sector into two groups: the "motivated seller" and everybody else. If the motivated seller dumps his government bond and bill holdings in exchange for other assets extremely rapidly, he will probably have to do so at "fire sale" prices relative to the financial assets that he is buying. If there are no other motivated sellers out there, the selling pressure will disappear, and the relative pricing will go back close to where it was before. This will result in (career-ending) catastrophic investment underperformance for the "motivated seller" versus his peers. Since the "motivated seller" does not know the true intentions of other market participants, the best course of action is to sell the bond position *quietly*. This prevents the out-of-control yield spiral that is the staple of bond market scare stories.

The requirement that everybody wants to get out of government debt—regardless of the yield—at the same time makes such a scenario unlikely. The belief that such scenarios are possible appears to be linked to models in which all trading in all markets (within an accounting period) occurs simultaneously.

There are a number of reasons why the belief that government will be able to roll over its debt represents a self-fulfilling outcome.

- It is not enough for selling to disrupt the bond market for a day or two; a well-run Treasury will have a balance at the central bank that covers its spending needs for a few months. All auctions over a period of weeks would have to fail completely, which gives the Treasury and central bank adequate time to find a solution.
- Primary dealers are *obligated* to bid at auction. This creates a community that has an interest in making sure that debt auctions succeed.
- For existing bondholders, the path of least resistance is to maintain their positions. "A rolling loan gathers no loss" is a popular saying amongst bankers because it has a large element of truth behind it.
- Government bonds are primarily held by institutional investors that have restrictions on the assets they can hold; typically, they must hold the bulk of their assets in investment grade debt.
- If the government defaults, it will likely take down other

entities that own government debt (such as banks). This means that there are no palatable alternatives to rotate into.

- Regulatory environments vary, but the local sovereign typically has a privileged position when it comes to bank regulatory requirements. Banks are free to pile up government debt on their balance sheet, without needing to held capital against it. This allows banks to speculate against government bond bears.
- Non-bank leveraged investors will be able to fund positions in short-term debt close to the policy rate, allowing them to accrue hefty profits if short-term yields are above the repo rate.[28]
- Finally, and most importantly, we need to look at the operations around bond auctions. Within the Simplified Framework, from the perspective of the private sector, a bond auction is an exchange of new bonds for old bonds. (If we allow for government lending, the private sector alternatively borrows from the government to buy the bonds.) As long as the new bonds are attractively priced relative to the old bonds, the auction will succeed. The bonds returned to the central bank could be longer maturity than the ones auctioned, reducing the perceived risk for the private sector.

All that needs to be done by the central bank is to set the interest rate paid on settlement balances at a level much lower than Treasury bill rates in order to drive banks into bills. For example, the central bank could set the interest rate on those balances to a negative level, and let banks trade off the possibility of a loss on a Treasury bill versus the guaranteed losses on the negative interest rate. In practice, such a draconian step is not necessary; setting the interest rate 25 basis points below the target rate is typically enough to keep banks holding Treasury bills.

Treasury debt management officials might argue that things are more complicated than this. I agree that their job is complicated, but that is because they have painted themselves into a very elaborate corner.

The central government is a monopoly supplier of government debt. One of the most basic concepts of a monopoly provider is that you can either set the price, or the quantity–but not both. For example, I am the

---

28   Warren Mosler describes how his fund did this in the section "Italian Epiphany" in Part 2 of *The Seven Deadly Frauds of Economic Policy.*

sole legal supplier of this report. I could emulate what is done with limited edition prints, and auction off a fixed number of copies. In this case, I am fixing the quantity, and the demand at the auction determines the price. On the other hand, I can do what I am doing: set the list price, and sell as many copies as are demanded at this price.[29] However, I cannot set the price and the quantity–if I could, it would be too easy for me to get rich.

Treasury officials have decided that they *must* auction fixed amounts of debt. They are thus forced to let the price (yield) float at auction. However, they also have an implicit price target as well–they do not want to pay "too much" interest. The thinking goes that if they pay "too much," that will be unacceptable, and they would be "forced" to default.

It is abundantly clear that a rigid Treasury could run into failed auctions if it is unwilling to adapt its auction schedule to market demand for debt. For example, if someone had the bright idea of only issuing 50-year bonds, the auctions would eventually fail (the banking system would not be allowed to buy large amounts of such debt). Therefore, "bond market vigilantes" could force a Treasury to rearrange its issuance plans, and force it to move towards shorter-maturities (where the central bank pins down yields). However, this is not enough to force default, assuming that the debt managers are halfway competent.

Finally, it should be noted that these mechanisms to prevent default assume that the central bank and the Treasury are looking to defend the national interest, and lean against any attempt by the private sector to force it into a default. It is entirely possible that these officials can be captured intellectually, and side with the market participants who believe that "market forces" should dictate fiscal policy. Nevertheless, the ability of these officials to force a default is limited, as the voters (and bondholders) would most likely crucify any political leader that allowed a default to occur.

6.7 Why Issue Bonds?

Given the somewhat vague nature of rollover risk, why not eliminate it? This is one of the recommendations of Modern Monetary Theory. It is straightforward for the government to stop issuing bonds, and eliminate the possibility of default. Although I agree that the MMT analysis is correct, in my view the elimination of rollover risk is easily done without elimi-

---

29   For legal reasons, I cannot set the retail price, only the list price.

nating bond issuance, and that there are costs to not having a bond market.

Why does the Treasury issue bonds in the first place (ignoring the Treasury balance issue)? The answer is that they act to keep interest rates away from zero. Most MMT analysis is discussed in the context of a banking system that uses reserves, and so bonds are termed a "reserve drain." If there are a lot excess reserves in the banking system (and if the Fed does not pay interest on reserves, which was the case until recently), the interbank rate would collapse to 0%. This would have meant that Federal Reserve would lose the ability to set interest rates above 0%.

If the government stopped issuing bonds, interest rates would drop to 0%, unless the central bank paid interest on settlement balances (reserves). (If the government pays interest on settlement balances, it is pretty much the same thing as having a bond market, in that the government still faces an interest bill that can be "too high." The usual MMT assumption is that the interest rate on reserves would be zero.)

A standard complaint about the abolition of the government bond market is that this would mean that there would be no benchmarks for pricing private debt. This would supposedly impair the functioning of the corporate debt markets. I do not think that this is too serious a complaint. The private sector can just switch over to price bonds off an interest rate swap curve.

Eliminating bond issuance would require some changes to operating procedures. In the absence of government bond auctions, there is no way for a Treasury to recharge its balance if it is running a fiscal deficit. Unless the central bank is literally consolidated into the Treasury, the Treasury would have to give itself the open-ended right to have an overdraft at the central bank. Although this might cause panic amongst some, it has no macroeconomic significance, as this is entirely an intra-government accounting issue.

Therefore, such a policy would be achievable, and we are already moving towards such a situation in the United States and Japan, as a result of the policy of Quantitative Easing (Section 5.4).

Nevertheless, I am unsure whether such a policy would gain much, while it would have some costs. The possibility of using interest rate policy to moderate the business cycle is lost. Although I do not believe that monetary policy is as powerful as mainstream economists suggest, there are cases where it is useful (such as moderating a housing boom). In addition, investors would lose the stabilising force of government bonds within their portfolios. As we saw in the Financial Crisis, only government bonds tend to increase in value when the private sector loses faith in the liquidity position of others. Hyman Minsky (amongst others) underlined the importance of government bonds for stabilising financial markets.

Meanwhile, it is easy to eliminate "rollover risk": the treasury just grants itself the right to run an open-ended overdraft at the central bank, and it limits the capacity of the central bank to set unreasonable rates on that overdraft. Once this is in place, there is no reason to fear default, and so the possibility of "rollover risk" disappears. The treasury could arrange its affairs exactly as before, not even needing to draw on the overdraft.

6.8 Concluding Remarks

Unlike a household or business, the government dictates the interest rate on its debt (albeit through the agency of the central bank, which is typically seen as independent). This means that government interest costs are largely self-determined, for the reason of the regulation of the economy. Although there is often speculation that the government will be unable to roll its debts, these fears seem to be misplaced. This speculation about the potential for governmental default is unnecessary, leading to the call by Modern Monetary Theory economists for the abolition of government debt.

Chapter 7 Domestic Constraints on Deficits

7.1 Introduction

If we grant the view that the government cannot be forced to default by markets, there does not appear to be any *financial* constraint upon government deficits. Although I believe that this is the correct view, that does not mean that there are no constraints whatsoever on government spending. Instead, the constraints show up on the "real side" of the economy: are government policies tying up "too much" of a nation's resources? The usual way in which this shows up is in the form of inflation: there is too much purchasing power in money terms for the amounts of goods and services being produced. This imbalance leads to rising prices of those goods and services, as well as wages. This trade-off became quite clear once the major economies left the Gold Standard, as the Gold Standard previously created financial limits on government policy. (I discuss such constraints in Chapter 8.) The school of thought that highlights this trade-off is known as Functional Finance.

Within mainstream economics, there is a tendency to reject Functional Finance principles. There is a belief that governments still face a financial constraint, which is known as the *inter-temporal governmental budget constraint* within economic models. Although the mathematics of this constraint is complex, I illustrate with simulation results why I believe that it is meaningless.

7.2 Functional Finance

Functional Finance is a body of thought that was originally proposed by the economist Abba P. Lerner. Functional Finance was associated with the Keynesian policies of the post-war era, but its influence eroded as Keynesian policies fell out of favour with the mainstream.[30] The idea is that you

30   Post-Keynesians argue that the economists that are commonly referred to as "Keynesian" were not in fact following the economic theory that was laid out by Keynes. However, that is how they were commonly described, and it is too late to change how they were labelled,

look at the function of fiscal policy (what it does), and ignore the form (such as the amount of budget balances, or how deficits are "financed").

Functional Finance is a key component of Modern Monetary Theory (MMT). In particular, MMT pays particular attention to monetary operations; the exact mechanisms of government finance. A central government that controls the currency that it issues debt in has a very different perspective on financing than a user of the currency, and this difference of perspective opens up the range of policies that may be attempted.

The principles of Functional Finance evolved over time, with developments added in response to the economic debates of the day. Since my objective is to explain the theoretical concepts, and not provide a history of economic thought, I will not attempt to cover the whole history of Functional Finance. Rather, I will focus on what I see as a defining work—"Functional Finance and the Federal Debt."[31]

Lerner summarises the philosophy of Functional Finance as:

> *The central idea is that government fiscal policy, its spending and taxing, its borrowing and repayment of loans, its issue of new money and its withdrawal of money, shall all be undertaken with an eye only to the results of these actions on the economy, and not to any established traditional doctrine about what is sound or unsound. The principle of judging only by the effects has been applied in many other fields of human activity, where it is known as the method of science as opposed to scholasticism. The principle of judging fiscal measures by the way they work or function in the economy we may call Functional Finance.*

What Lerner refers to as "sound finance" is also known as the Treasury View, or the loanable funds doctrine. (The name the Treasury View came from the fact that it was best summarised by the staff of the British Chancellor of the Exchequer, the equivalent of the U.S. Treasury, when they explained why counter-cyclical fiscal policy was futile during the Great Depression.)

Within the article, Lerner describes two laws of Functional Finance. (I am summarising these laws using more familiar terms.)

---

as that school of thought no longer really exists. There is also an argument that the high inflation of the 1970s (which damaged the political credibility of Keynesian policies) was not the result of Keynesian economic principles, but rather a botched response to an oil price shock.

31   *Functional Finance and the Federal Debt*, Abba Lerner, Social Research 10: 38-51, 1943.

1. The first responsibility of the government is to adjust aggregate demand with either taxes or spending so that the economy is running at potential without causing inflationary pressures.
2. The government should only issue debt if it is desirable to change the mix between money and government debt holdings within the non-government sector. This is done to adjust rates of interest.

The second law of Functional Finance is the source of the viewpoint that states, "government bonds are a reserve drain." Since that was already discussed in Section 5.3, I will now focus on the first law and its relevance to the analysis of fiscal policy.

One implication of the first law drawn by Lerner is that "taxing is never to be undertaken merely because the government needs to make money payments." In other words, citizens do not pay tax because the government "needs the money." This point of view does not match the standard intuition that taxes are needed to fund government spending.

The way I interpret his statement is as follows. We know that the government will typically run deficits year after year, just to keep the level of debt stable relative to nominal GDP, which normally grows. Therefore, we expect that in each year, there is a mismatch in dollar amounts between spending and taxes. Since this mismatch will always persist (as I will discuss in Section 7.5, which discusses whether government debt will be "paid back"), there is no way to directly link any particular spending programme with tax revenues. This is unlike the situation for an individual, where all spending has to come out of existing financial resources or debt, and that debt is dealt with either during the individual's lifetime or by that person's estate.

I am somewhat cautious in advancing this principle. It does not mean that taxes can be abolished; they are needed to contain inflationary pressures. Nevertheless, it does point us in an interesting direction–since different taxes have a different effect on demand for the same dollar amount of taxes raised, you cannot assess the stance of fiscal policy solely by looking at the aggregate amount of taxes raised. Instead, the mix of taxes and spending matters. Correspondingly, we cannot conclude too much about the stance of fiscal policy solely by looking at the size of the fiscal deficit.

Additionally, the first law implies that inflation is heavily influenced by fiscal policy. I believe that this is largely correct in terms of the broad trend in inflation, but it does not mean that we can look at fiscal policy and use it to forecast the wiggles in inflation. Since the early 1990s, fiscal policy settings in most countries have been relatively stable, and so the business cycle (and inflation) has largely reflected shifting confidence within the private sector.

An important statement within the paper is "Functional Finance rejects completely the traditional doctrines of 'sound finance' and the principle of trying to balance the budget over a solar year or any other arbitrary period." Given the fad for embracing balanced budgets on either an annual basis (or using vague periods like "across the cycle"), this is a component of Functional Finance that mainstream thought appears to have rejected.

However, even this rejection is less serious than it appears. Most observers discuss the value of stabilising debt/GDP ratios at various levels, such as the 60% of GDP level that made its way into the Maastricht Treaty. There is little discussion of driving debt/GDP ratios to zero, other than by those who insist that government debt "must be paid back" (discussed further in Section 7.5). As long as nominal GDP is rising, simple mathematics tells us that balanced budgets across any fixed cycle would in fact drive the debt-to-GDP ratio to zero. Since this would be obviously problematic, most "balanced budget" proposals contain holes that exclude "good" categories of spending from the budget balance constraint, such as "investment." Since practically any government spending can be reclassified by a good spin doctor as being "investment," there is no real constraint on net government spending.

This treatment of this topic is brief. For further information, I recommend "Functional Finance: What, Why and How?" by Stephanie Kelton (née Bell).[32]

7.3 Mainstream Analysis of Government Financing

The mainstream approach to governmental finances revolves around two sets of equations, or constraints, which describe the financial position of the government. The first describes the accounting of government debt;

---

32   Bell, Stephanie, *Functional Finance: What, Why, and How?* (November 1999). Levy Economics Institute Working Paper No. 287. Available at SSRN: http://ssrn.com/abstract=199971 or http://dx.doi.org/10.2139/ssrn.199971

the second is a constraint on the future path of the fiscal balance. The accounting equations are innocuous, but the constraint on the fiscal balance is highly problematic. I will briefly comment in the accounting identity within this section, and then turn to the fiscal balance constraint in the next section.

The accounting identity is based on the following observation:

(Fiscal deficit) = (Increase in Government Liabilities) = (Increase in Debt) + (Increase in Money).

(There is a slight technical issue around the definition of the increase in debt, as the usual formulation within mainstream models has the government issuing Treasury bills. The increase in debt within the equation is the increase in market value of government debt. The increase in the face value of debt is larger, as Treasury bills are issued at a discount.)

This equation is then reformulated as:

Government Spending = (Taxes) + (Increase in Debt) + (Increase in Money).

This statement is then interpreted as—"government spending is financed either by taxes, debt, or money issuance." This then leads to discussions about how government spending can have different effects depending upon whether it is financed by debt, money, or taxes. That is, the argument is that there is a definite tie between any government programme and by the means of financing it.

In my view, these discussions are largely hand-waving fables; they do not correspond to any reputable theory. Reviewing how government operations work as seen in Chapter 4, all government spending is "financed" by the government writing a cheque. Money is only issued if the private sector wishes to withdraw currency, which is independent of government spending. Debt issuance is a separate activity, used to replenish the Treasury's balance, and/or drain reserves (if they exist). Taxes are needed to provide a demand for currency to support the domestic price level, and the relationship between any particular spending programme and taxation may be very slight.

It is not an exaggeration to say that MMT authors have been exasperated by the sloppy thinking that the mainstream interpretation of the accounting identity has spawned. As a result, they are highly allergic to people using the term "financing" with respect to government spending.

7.4 The Governmental Budget Constraint

The modern mainstream approach to macroeconomics revolves around the use of Dynamic Stochastic General Equilibrium (DSGE) models. These models are the object of controversy, and they are particularly opposed by *heterodox* economists, such as post-Keynesians. I am not going to discuss this wider controversy; rather I wish to discuss the concept of the *inter-temporal governmental budget constraint*, which I will also refer to here as the "governmental budget constraint." This is tied to the notion of *fiscal sustainability*, in that any "fiscal policy rule"[33] is allegedly sustainable if and only if it meets the inter-temporal governmental budget constraint.

There are a great many types of DSGE models, and it should be noted that not all of them refer to the governmental budget constraint discussed within this section. As a result, the statements made here do not apply to *all* DSGE models; in fact, variations of some of the criticisms here have appeared within the DSGE literature.[34] That said, other types of DSGE models without this budget constraint could have other shortcomings in their treatment of fiscal policy.

In its simplest form, the inter-temporal governmental budget constraint can be written without mathematical notation as:

(Market Value of Government Debt) = (Discounted sum of all future primary fiscal balances).

The *primary fiscal balance* is the fiscal balance excluding interest payments. Stripping interest payments out of the fiscal balance only appears to make

---

33   One of the complications of DSGE models is that they are specified in terms of the expected future path of the economy. Therefore, we cannot just specify current fiscal policy, we need to specify the expected path of fiscal policy, which can only be done by developing some form of rule it will follow.
34   The best-known examples are Overlapping Generations (OLG) models. The reason why the governmental budget constraint is not believed to hold in this case is the result of there being an infinite number of households within the model. The most introductory explanation of fiscal policy within DSGE models that I have found is in Chapter 12 of the text *Advanced Macroeconomics* (Fourth Edition), by David Romer, McGraw-Hill, 2008. That text is aimed at first-year graduate students, so the complexity of the analysis is much greater than this report.

senseif we assume that monetary policy (which determines interest payments) and fiscal policy can be decoupled, an assumption that appears dubious.

Please note that in some treatments, the governmental budget constraint may be defined as the above relationship along with the accounting identity discussed in the previous section. I do not include it in my discussion here, as it is obviously correct. (A mathematician would describe it as "trivially true.")

Additionally, the formulation above ignores how money affects government finance through "seigneurage revenue" (defined in Section 4.2). This is often ignored in DSGE models, as those models implicitly assume that nobody holds money (as that would be suboptimal behaviour). I will discuss this complication later.

Example. *Imagine that we have a country with $100 in debt outstanding in Year 0. Assume that the debt entirely consists of 1-year bills, and that the interest rate is 5% for all time. The primary balance is $0 in Year 0.*

1. *After one year, the debt will have compounded to $105. If the government wishes to pay back its debt, it would have to run a primary surplus of $105 ($100 plus the $5 interest on the debt accrued in Year 0). Since the debt is paid back completely, there is no interest expense after Year 1. A $105 primary surplus in Year 1 has a discounted value of $100 (=$105/1.05), and the primary surplus is $0 for all other years. The sum of the discounted fiscal balances is $100, which is the market value of the debt in Year 0.*

2. *Alternatively, assume the government pays back the debt in Year 2, while it has a primary balance of $0 in every other year. The debt will have compounded to a value of $110.25, ($5 interest in Year 1, and $5.25 in Year 2). The present value of $110.25 in 2 years is $100 (=$110.25/((1.05)×(1.05))), which is once again equal to the initial market value of the debt.*

As discussed below, it is not necessary for the government to pay back its debt, but the calculations are more difficult to write out. The results for these more complicated cases are demonstrated graphically below.

For simplicity, I will assume that the economy is in *a steady state,* in which nominal interest rates and nominal GDP growth rates are constant.[35] Within a DSGE model, this assumption is too restrictive, but we

---

35   This may not match the intuition of a steady state from physics, but it is used in stock-flock consistent (SFC) models. In a steady state, economic aggregates grow at the same rate, and so ratios of such variables are constant.

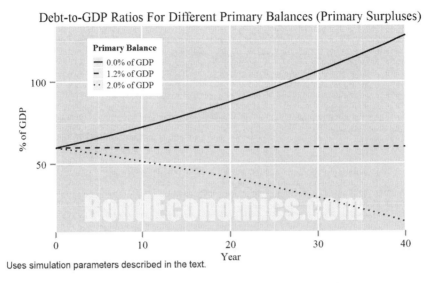

Debt-to-GDP Ratios For Different Primary Balances (Primary Surpluses)

Uses simulation parameters described in the text.

Figure 13. *Debt-to-GDP ratio depending upon growth rates*

can extend the analysis to the more general case at the cost of complexity.[36]

For now, we will assume that the interest rate on debt is greater than the growth rate of nominal GDP. This is an important assumption with regard to the governmental budget constraint. If the interest rate is lower than the growth rate of GDP, the picture is quite different, as discussed in Section 7.6.

Figure 13 shows how the debt-to-GDP ratio evolves for a set of scenarios. In each scenario, nominal GDP grows at 4% per year, whereas the interest rate on debt is 6%. I assume that money balances are zero. The initial value of government debt represents 60% of GDP. The topmost line shows what happens if the primary surplus is held at 0% of GDP at all times: the debt-to-GDP ratio continues to grow without bound.

The middle line is what happens if the primary surplus is 1.2% of GDP: the debt-to-GDP ratio remains constant at 60% of GDP. Please note that in this case there is a total fiscal deficit at all times, but it only

36   Instead of assuming that growth rates are constant, we can bound the actual trajectory between two trajectories that have growth rates that are above and below the "long-term" growth rate. As long as nominal GDP growth rates do not become unbounded ("tend to infinity") this can always be done. If the growth rate does tend to infinity, we are in the realm of an "unsustainable trajectory."

allows the debt stock to grow at 4% per year, which is below the rate of interest. This illustrates the important property that continuous deficits are needed to stabilise the debt-to-GDP ratio if the economy is growing in nominal terms. This has the implication that balanced budgets are associated with a debt-to-GDP ratio converging towards zero, which would be problematic for the operation of the financial system.

The bottom series depicts what happens if the surplus is larger than the stabilising 1.2% of GDP level: the debt-to-GDP ratio continuously falls, and would eventually become negative.

The top trajectory and the bottom both represent "unsustainable" debt trajectories. If the government tried to force its debt stock to be negative (somehow), the banking system would cease to function given the lack of position-making instruments. The usual worry, however, is a debt-to-GDP ratio that becoming arbitrarily large. If this were projected to happen, bondholders would presumably be nervous about owning bonds, as they will presumably become worthless at some point. The debate however, is whether such an outcome could be achieved, and the post-Keynesian position is very simple: such an out-of-control spiral would not happen in practice, and this tells us very little about fiscal policy. Mainstream models do not specify fiscal policy correctly, and the possibility of a "debt spiral" is just a *degenerate*[37] outcome that is the result of model misspecification. It is true that the budget constraint relation holds (under the assumption about the interest rate being higher than the growth rate). The issue is how to interpret it.

7.5 Paying the Debt Back?

One popular interpretation of the budget constraint is that "the government will have to pay back its debt." This is a formulation that is often seen in internet discussion, which seems to imply that the government must drive the debt-to-GDP ratio to zero. *This is not true.* A fiscal trajectory meets the constraint so long as *any* upper limit to the debt-to-GDP ratio time series exists. The ratio could drift towards 10,000%, and the trajectory is "sustainable" on this measure.

The reason why you need a positive primary fiscal balance (a *pri-*

---

37   I am using *degenerate* in a formal sense that is used by mathematicians; ithe model is technically correct, but the results make no sense.

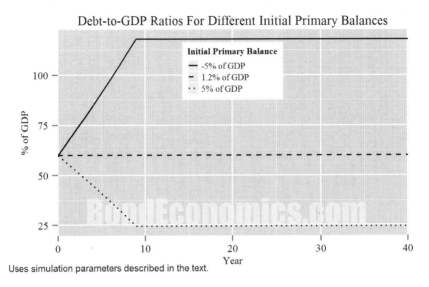

Uses simulation parameters described in the text.

Figure 14. *Debt-to-GDP ratios for scenarios*

mary surplus) is that you need to apply a brake to the debt dynamics in order prevent the debt-to-GDP ratio from going to infinity (assuming that the interest rate is greater than the growth rate of the economy). If you set the primary surplus such that the debt-to-GDP ratio is constant (that is, debt grows at the same rate as GDP), the present value of the series will equal the market value of the debt.

More generally, you could run a smaller surplus for a period, and then enter a steady state primary balance in which the debt-to-GDP ratio remains constant at a higher level. The initially smaller surpluses will be balanced by higher surpluses later, since the higher debt-to-GDP ratio requires a larger primary balance to reach the steady growth condition. Despite the extra dynamics, the constraint equation still holds. In this manner, we can steer the debt-to-GDP ratio to any positive level, remain there, and still satisfy the constraint.

Example. *There are three scenarios (Figure 14), with the same parameters for the growth rate (4%) and interest rate (6%). The difference is that this time, the primary balance is set to a particular percentage of GDP for the first 10 years (Years 0-9 on the chart), and then the primary balance reverts to a level that is consistent with a constant debt-to-GDP ratio. The initial primary balances for the scenarios are -5%, 1.2%, and 5% of GDP.*

Figure 15 shows the path of primary balances. The trajectory that starts with a

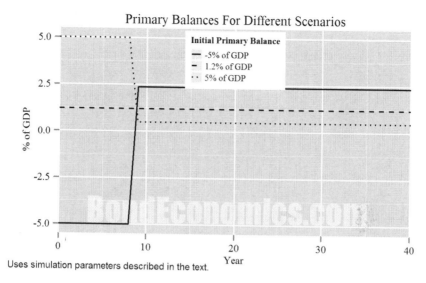

Figure 15. *Primary balances for scenarios*

large primary deficit (-5% of GDP) switches over to having the largest primary balance in Year 10, almost 2.5% of GDP. The scenario that starts with large surpluses (5% of GDP) drops off to the smallest primary balance, as the debt-to-GDP ratio has been crushed down and a smaller surplus is needed to stabilise the debt-to-GDP ratio.

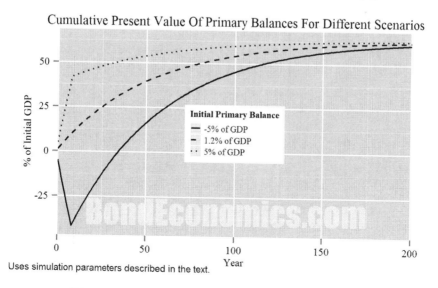

Figure 16. *Sum of primary balances over time for scenarios*

Figure 16 on page 71 shows the cumulative discounted values of the primary surpluses for each scenario. (For each year, we calculate the dollar value of the primary balance, and then discount it by the interest rate factor [1.06] raised to the power of the number of years in the future. We then add up all of these discounted balances. For example, the value at Year 50 is the sum of the discounted balances from years 0-50.) In all cases, the cumulative discounted surpluses converge towards the market value of the initial amount of debt outstanding, which is 60% of GDP in Year 0. This convergence will hold for any trajectory that has the debt-to-GDP ratio stabilising at a limit that is greater than or equal to zero.

Therefore, we cannot say the "debt will be paid back," other than the trivial observation that individual bond issues are paid off as they mature, while the stock of debt is steadily increasing.

All the governmental budget constraint says is that for every dollar in debt, the government will need to run a future primary surplus that has a discounted value (present value) of $1, under the strong assumption that the rate of compounding on government debt is greater than the growth rate of the economy.

Within DSGE models that are based upon a hypothetical infinitely long-lived representative household,[38] the implication is that for every dollar in government debt (per household), the household will get a future tax bill that is worth $1 now. This supposedly will cause the household to increase savings to be able to pay the future tax. The result is that deficit spending will not stimulate activity, as it will be met by increased household savings. (This assertion about household behaviour is known as *Ricardian Equivalence*.) This topic is rather complex and controversial; I would summarise my position by saying that this argument about household behaviour does not appear to match real-world data.

7.6 Complications with the Budget Constraint

There are a number of difficulties with the governmental budget constraint as it is typically presented. Some are technical issues that could be dealt with by small adjustments, but there is a critical problem: the assumption that the nominal growth rate of the economy is less than the discount rate may in fact not hold. The mathematical expression completely breaks down if this assumption is violated.

---

38   Yes, that sounds completely crazy.

I will now outline four issues with the budget constraint.

1. Money. The definition for the budget constraint I used assumed that there is no money (which pays interest at a 0% rate) within the economy. This is obviously incorrect. There are two possible fixes. The first way is to add corrections to the mathematical expression for "seigneurage revenue." The new version of the equation is:

Present Value of Debt = Sum of Discounted (Primary Balances + Seigneurage Revenue).

This leads to a complex-looking equation, and is hard to interpret. The second way to fix the problem is to describe the budget constraint in terms of government liabilities (money and debt), and then the interest rate used is the effective interest rate on liabilities; which is the weighted average of the interest rate on the debt and the interest on money (0%). This has the effect that the effective interest rate on all government liabilities is below the interest on government bonds and bills.

2. **Taxes on Interest.** The decomposition of the fiscal balance into the primary balance plus interest expense is designed to make the primary balance as positive as possible. Interest expense is taken away, but the taxes paid on interest are not. An increase in the interest paid will be partially balanced by the increase in taxes paid by bondholders, and the government need not change any other policy setting. Therefore, a more reasonable version of this constraint would only deduct the after-tax interest expense from the fiscal balance. This means that the appropriate interest rate to be used in (modified) equation is the after-tax interest rate, which is also lower than the unadjusted interest rate.

3. Term Premium. This factor is more complex, but it also leads to a lower effective interest rate. The discount rate used within the intertemporal budget constraint is defined by long-term bond yields. However, governments typically issue a large weighting of short-dated securities, such as Treasury bills. Those Treasury bills can be rolled over at an interest rate that is typically lower than the long-term bond yield. This has the result that the rate of compounding of debt is lower than what is implied by the discount rate. This is because there is a "term premium" in long-term bond yields. (That is, they have higher yields than the expected return on rolling over Treasury bills.) A significant portion of modern portfolio allocation theory assumes that this term premium is positive. This issue is not highly publicised, but I discussed it in article on my web site.[39]

4. Growth Rate Higher than the Discount Rate. This is the most crippling problem the budget constraint equation faces. If the nominal growth rate of the economy is greater than the nominal long-term bond yield, there is no good reason for the constraint to hold.[40] The constraint implies that the growth rate of debt is less than the rate of interest, which means the amount of debt is growing less than GDP. This implies that the debt-to-GDP ratio will go to 0% as time increases. This makes little sense, as the lack of government debt will cripple the functioning of the financial system.

The importance of this factor is magnified by the fact that the previous three factors act to lower the effective interest rate paid on debt. This increases the chance that the nominal GDP growth rate is greater than the effective interest rate paid on debt.

If we instead allow the debt-to-GDP ratio to not converge towards zero, the budget constraint equation within DSGE models no longer converges (under the assumption of GDP growth greater than the discount rate). From the point of view of a mathematician, the system of equations that define the DSGE model become nonsensical, and there is no solution. The model economy disappears in a puff of mathematical contradiction. To complicate matters, the discount rate and the growth rate of the economy depend upon the solution of the model, as the economic outcome is supposed to be the result of the optimising choice of an economic agent. How an agent can optimise over choices when most of the sensible economic trajectories do not exist is very unclear. This topic is difficult to explain, as the DSGE literature is muddled. Economists have a very cavalier attitude towards assuming that solutions to the models that they write down exist and are unique, which is completely unlike how dynamical

---

39   *What Is Ricardian Equivalence, And Why It Does Not Hold*, Brian Romanchuk, December 7, 2013. URL: *http://www.bondeconomics.com/2013/12/what-is-ricardian-equivalence-and-why.html*

40   There is a microeconomic story behind the constraint in this case, related to a concept known as the "no Ponzi" condition. I believe that the logic in this microeconomic argument is incorrect, but a proof of my statement is well beyond the scope of this report. For now, it is enough to reject the condition on the practical basis that the debt-to-GDP ratio must go to zero if it were true.

systems are approached by applied mathematicians in other fields.

7.7 Can We Model Fiscal Constraints?

The desire of the users of DSGE models is to summarise fiscal policy as a fixed constraint, so that attention can then be turned to monetary policy (which they assume as being more important). As we have seen, the budget constraint used is meaningless, if not incorrect. Can we find another relationship which acts as the limit of what represents sustainable fiscal policy?

The answer appears to be: not easily. In order to decide whether fiscal policy is "sustainable," we can only define this within the context of the dynamics of the model. From the standpoint of Functional Finance, fiscal policy settings are "sustainable" so long as they do not cause unwanted inflation. The problem is that there is no consensus on the relationship between fiscal policy and inflation. In extreme cases, there is some agreement—running a fiscal deficit of 50% of GDP under peacetime conditions[41] is likely to cause extreme inflation if not hyperinflation. However, if we look at the modern developed economies, there is little consensus as to what has been driving inflation over recent decades.

The post-1990s period has seen stable inflation in the developed markets (even if there have been periodic outbursts of instability within the financial and credit markets). However, this inflation stability has coincided with large swings in debt-to-GDP ratios. Japan provides an extreme case for this. Correspondingly, there is no simple rule that relates fiscal deficits to inflation trends.[42] We need to take into account other factors within the economy.

The desire to accumulate financial assets within the private sector is

---

41   During World War II, most of the combatants' governments essentially took over the economy (if they had not done so already, as was the case in Germany and the Soviet Union). It was possible to run very large fiscal deficits without extreme inflation, as goods were controlled by rationing. Such a system is very different from the peacetime capitalist economies that I am focussing on here.

42   There is "the Fiscal Theory of the Price Level," which does imply a simple relationship between inflation and fiscal policy. The problem with this theory is that it is too simple, and generates strong predictions about the price level. It is unclear that observed inflation data match the predictions of the theory.

one such factor. It is almost completely ignored within mainstream analysis. However, if private sector entities want to accumulate large stocks of safe financial assets, and there is no entity that is willing or able to provide such assets, something has to give. The way in which modern welfare states operate is that the "automatic stabilisers" deal with this mismatch between the demand and supply for safe assets. Nominal GDP growth slows, which has two effects upon the fiscal balance.

1. Nominal incomes are lower than expected, which lowers the amount of taxes paid relative to projections.
2. Slower growth raises unemployment rates, which will induce extra unemployment insurance and welfare payments.

These automatic adjustments occur because of changing activity. The rapid rise in fiscal deficits during the Financial Crisis was largely the result of these automatic factors; discretionary changes added to the deficits, but were generally smaller in magnitude.

This gives a much different view of the path of the debt-to-GDP ratio in the United States since the 1990s. (Other countries had similar experiences.) The U.S. economy grew steadily during the two decades before the Financial Crisis, other than the recession triggered by the meltdown of the technology bubble in 2000. That recession was relatively mild—at least outside of the technology sector. During this period, the private sector emitted a great deal of debt. Private sector debt replaced government bonds on investor balance sheets, making room for a lower Federal debt-to-GDP ratio. When private sector debt creation was impaired during the Financial Crisis, Federal Government debt was needed to provide the financial assets needed for private portfolios.

The justification for this interpretation of economic history requires delving deeper into post-Keynesian economic modelling. My remarks above are based upon the models found in the following papers.

1. "Interest Rates and Fiscal Sustainability," by Scott T. Fullwiler.[43]
2. "Fiscal Policy in a Stock-Flow Consistent (SFC) Model," by Wynne Godley and Marc Lavoie.[44]

43   Fullwiler, Scott T., *Interest Rates and Fiscal Sustainability* (July 1, 2006). Available at SSRN: http://ssrn.com/abstract=1722986 or http://dx.doi.org/10.2139/ssrn.1722986

44   This article is in the book *The Stock-Flow Consistent Approach: Selected*

One of the implications of the analysis by Godley, Lavoie, and Fullwiler is that debt spirals are unlikely in practice. The private sector will adjust its behaviour in response to holding higher levels of government debt, and start to spend more out of its income. This will raise nominal activity (possibly in the form of inflation), which will tend to lower the budget deficit. The exact response depends upon the form of the model, and there is little consensus about those model parameters. That said, many conventional treatments implicitly assume that the private sector will not adjust behaviour at all in response to increased financial asset holdings, which appears unreasonable.

7.8 Concluding Remarks

The inter-temporal governmental budget constraint is either trivial or wrong. If we are in a situation where the expected interest rate is higher than the expected growth rate of the economy, all it implies is that the debt-to-GDP ratio will "not go to infinity." We have very good reasons to believe that was the case already, even in the absence of the constraint. Conversely, if the expected interest rate is too low, it implies that the debt-to-GDP ratio will go to zero. This is incompatible with the proper functioning of a financial sector that is dependent upon the use of government debt for liquidity management purposes.

As Abba Lerner recognised, the true constraint on fiscal policy is inflation, not financial. Unfortunately, we do not have reliable models of the drivers of inflation, so we do not have a precise idea where the limits on fiscal policy lie.

Writings of Wynne Godley, edited by Marc Lavoie and Gennaro Zezza. Published by Palgrave Macmillan, 2012.

Chapter 8 Outside Constraints on Governments

8.1 Introduction

Although I have described a system in which government default is voluntary and presumably rare, the historical record is full of government defaults. The explanation for this is that governments historically bound themselves with external constraints in their operating procedures. Within the developed countries, various forms of the Gold Standard acted as the main constraint. After the demise of the Bretton Woods system, defaults have largely been associated with countries that borrow in a foreign currency, or peg the value of their currency to another (typically the U.S. dollar). The euro area is an elaborate system of exchange rate pegs that are disguised as a single currency, and is in danger of unravelling at the time of writing.

This chapter discusses such constraints that have been imposed by governments. Section 8.6 discusses sub-sovereign governments, such as cities, Provinces or States. Although they are governments, they operate within a monetary system that is defined by the central government. This means that they have a great deal of similarities to households or corporates, despite the superficial similarity of accounting between the levels of government.

8.2 Borrowing in Foreign Currency

One of the working assumptions within this report is that the government is not borrowing in a foreign currency. This is a practice that is common in developing countries (or at least it was), but is rare amongst the developed ones in the post-World War II era. (The euro area countries do not count under this definition; they do not control the euro, but it is the local currency. The problem in the euro area is the practice of currency pegging, which is discussed in the next section.) This practice explains why sovereign default is common in the developing countries, but not the developed ones.

Since the currency of borrowing is not the local currency, the description of operations in Chapter 4 no longer applies. The borrowing nation is in the same boat as others, such as corporations.

There is the risk that domestic firms may borrow in foreign currencies, and their failure may drag down the sovereign, even if it has no foreign currency borrowing itself. This sort of behaviour was behind the Asian Crisis of 1997 (and the collapse of the Icelandic banking system), but this behaviour is relatively rare in the richer developed countries.

8.3 Gold Parities and Currency Pegs

Other than foreign currency borrowing, the most typical cause in a breakdown of government finance is a policy of pegging the currency to an external instrument, such as gold or a foreign currency. The study of financial history before the 1970s is largely the study of the crises spawned by fixed exchange rate regimes. After the demise of the Bretton Woods system, developed countries moved towards floating exchange rates–other than European nations, which stubbornly continue to enter fixed exchange rate arrangements. For these countries, periodic crises have been the norm, including the demise of "the Snake" (1970s), the ejection of Britain from the ERM (1992), and the current crisis in the Eurozone (2010-present).

In a gold or currency peg, a government promises to keep the price of an external asset (gold or foreign currency) at a fixed price versus the local currency. This fixed price is often referred to as a "parity," so one sees statements like "the government intervened to defend its gold parity."

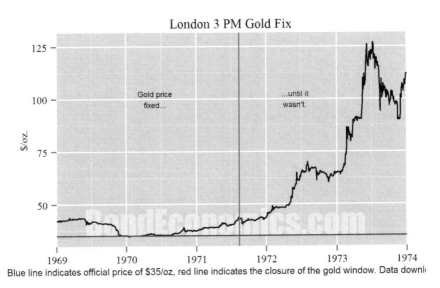

Blue line indicates official price of $35/oz, red line indicates the closure of the gold window. Data downl

Figure 17. *Gold price at the end of the Bretton Woods system*

This promise is backed up by a promise to redeem the local currency in exchange for the external asset. (The details vary by case; for example, under the Bretton Woods system, only foreign governments could exchange U.S. dollars for gold.) For simplicity, I will discuss a gold peg herein; the mechanics of an exchange rate peg are fundamentally similar, but the details of implementation are often more complex.

In terms of monetary operations, this adds a new way in which the government interacts with the non-government sector. It is now possible for the private sector to exchange government bonds (or currency) for gold, or vice-versa.

Why do gold pegs fail? The government can always issue new bonds in exchange for gold, as these securities are electronic entries and are essentially costless to create. The problem occurs when the government is called upon to redeem bonds or money in exchange for gold. The amount of government money is typically larger than what is implied by the amount of gold outstanding (and even more if you add in bonds).

For example, assume that the monetary base was twice what is "covered" by gold. If there were a rush to redeem money, it would only take redemption of half of the monetary base to liquidate the government's total gold holdings. The remaining money would be left "uncovered" completely. This creates a self-fulfilling run on gold; you want to get your gold before the government runs out. Governments historically either suspended gold redemption or changed the gold parity. If other countries have fixed pegs to gold, this devalues the currency versus those peers.

Currency pegs are incompatible with fractional reserve banking; since the government only covers a portion of the monetary base, and bank deposits ("bank money") is a multiple of the monetary base, a run on bank money is always possible. Runs on banking systems are a typical trigger for problems for currency pegs.

A gold parity or a peg to a foreign currency is a promise that cannot always be kept, as governments cannot create gold or foreign currencies out of thin air. When analysing a sovereign with such a promise outstanding, you have to monitor whether it has the capacity to keep its promise (like any other borrower).

As a final note, the problems in the Euro area can be traced to the reality that it is a currency peg system. The national currencies were supposedly eliminated and replaced by "euros," but the reality is that only the euro currency notes are common instruments. The national banking systems still exist under the hood. Although all euros were supposed to be the same, Greek and Cypriot euros were in fact not truly fungible, as they are tied to their national banking systems. Within the euro zone, the TARGET2 system is a clearing system that is supposed to ensure that the underlying national currencies would trade at a 1:1 exchange rate. If there is a payment imbalance between countries, the mismatch morphs into an imbalance between the national central banks within the TARGET2 system. The survival of the exchange rate peg is the willingness of surplus countries to lend to the deficit countries within this system. At the time of writing, the TARGET2 system has not yet buckled, but it will face considerable pressure during the next widespread economic slowdown.

8.4 One-Sided Currency Pegs

There is a more viable version of a currency peg–a one-sided peg. The government does not guarantee that the currency will not be too cheap versus an external currency, but it does its best to prevent the currency from becoming too strong. Since a government can create its currency without requiring real resources, such a policy appears sustainable.

Many countries have pursued policies similar to one-sided pegs as a developmental strategy in the post-World War II era. Germany and Japan were early successes. They used relatively cheap currencies to power an export boom to the United States as a means of raising business sector profits, allowing them to become manufacturing powerhouses. In later decades, this policy was pursued by other Asian countries, with the most remarkable example being China.

However, this policy of keeping the currency cheap was usually attempted in an environment where the financial sector was tightly controlled, as well as international financial transactions (capital controls). The use of these controls allowed the countries to avoid some of the inflationary effects of the weak currency policy, as well as limiting private sector speculation against the value of the currency.

Japan is somewhat unusual within the developed countries for its policy of large foreign exchange interventions within a financial system that lacks capital controls. The Japanese do not announce particular targets for the yen, but rather seem to want to push

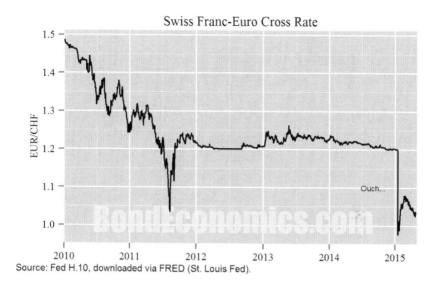

Figure 18. *Swiss-Euro exchange rate and the one-sided peg*

the yen from becoming "too strong." Since there are no particular levels it wants to defend, this was only a "soft peg." This flexibility reduces the instability of markets attacking particular currency levels.

However, some developed countries have had harder versions of a one-sided peg. One recent example was the Swiss National Bank's policy of preventing the Swiss franc from strengthening below 1.20 francs per euro. (A lower value for the euro/franc exchange rate means a stronger franc versus the euro.) Even so, the Swiss National Bank (SNB) was forced to retreat from that policy in January 2015 (Figure 18). The policy required the SNB to make large purchases of euro-denominated government bonds, and it came under increasing political pressure as the result of the growth of the size of its balance sheet.

In summary, a one-sided peg may be financially sustainable, but there may be side effects that make it *politically* unsustainable. Since it is difficult to determine what the political limits for these side effects are, it is harder to forecast when a one-sided peg will be abandoned.

8.5 External Constraints without a Currency Peg

Even if there is no currency peg in place, countries still have to be mindful of the external value of the currency (how much it is worth versus other currencies). Moreover, if the country runs persistent current account deficits, it is likely that foreigners are accumulating large financial asset holdings in the domestic economy (further explanation[45]). These capital flows could reverse if foreigners lose confidence in the value of domestic financial assets, causing a crisis in the financial markets and a crash in the currency. Another concern is the buildup of government bond holdings by foreigners—can they veto fiscal policy by threatening to sell their positions? These concerns appear to form an "external constraint" on domestic policy.

Such external crises are common in emerging markets, even in nations where the currency was free floating. They also used to plague the United Kingdom, which struggled with a continuously overvalued exchange rate. Such episodes are largely non-existent for the developed countries with free-floating currencies (which only covers the post-1970s era).

In my view, a few factors distinguish the fortunes of the developed countries versus the others.

- The developed countries have large, highly integrated corporate equities markets. Equity investors typically do not hedge their currency exposure, and so they have the capacity to lean against rapid currency movements.
- Developed countries feature large financial sectors, which hold large stocks of financial assets (for example, pension funds). These investors wish to meet domestic currency liability benchmarks, and so they will have a tendency to return capital home when the local currency weakens. In many developing countries, by contrast, financial assets are largely held by rich individuals who have a tendency to flee the local economy when it is under pressure.
- A significant portion of cross-border trade in the developed

---

45   The current account deficit is the trade deficit plus the deficit in cross-country income transfers (neglecting small terms in the international transaction accounts). If a country is running a current account deficit, it is a net importer, and it cannot pay for those imports with external income flows. Therefore, it has to be transferring financial assets to the exporters in some fashion (that is, the current account deficit must be financed). The financing could be in the form of foreigners buying domestic assets, locals selling foreign assets, or locals borrowing in a foreign currency.

world is actually internal trade within corporations. The transfer pricing within corporate units is somewhat arbitrary, as evidenced by the fact that almost all of the profits of multinational corporations are attributed to low-tax jurisdictions. Since this cross border trade is administered at the convenience of the corporation, it can choose to ignore currency movements that it feels are temporary.

- Consumers in the developed countries mainly spend their money on highly processed foods and services, which are largely insulated from the effect of exchange rate moves. For example, consumer price inflation trends are similar on both sides of the Canada-United States border since the early 1990s, yet the Canadian dollar has had very large swings versus the U.S. dollar over that period. Consumers in developing countries typically have a high weight of unprocessed food items in their household spending, and those unprocessed foods are more exposed to foreign exchange movements.

- The developed economies have highly productive agricultural sectors (which are protected behind strong regulatory walls) which produce staples, while many developing economies have been pushed towards cash crops. This makes those developing countries more vulnerable to currency shifts.

Taken together, these factors make the developed countries robust to exchange rate movements. This allows policymakers to pursue a policy of "benign neglect" towards the currency. The Japanese government has the most activist foreign exchange policy (outside of Europe), and even there, the currency has had extremely wide swings since the mid-1990s without any noticeable effect on the price level.

The much-discussed issue of foreign ownership of government bonds also does not seem to have much of a visible effect. This is because foreign holders of government bonds have no special privileges vis-à-vis domestic holders of government debt. Since there is no mechanism to convert local currency to foreign currency (like in a currency peg), the local currency forms a closed system. If foreigners want to get out of the local currency, they need to find a buyer that is willing to exchange that currency for another. Doing such exchanges at fire sale prices is a good way to destroy the value of your portfolio, which is why most large investors avoid panicking whenever possible.

Nevertheless, there are some more subtle issues involved with the external constraint. The concern is that if the government runs too stimulative a policy, it will raise imports and the current account deficit will widen. Moreover, a falling currency would augment the inflationary effect of the stimulative policies.

I believe that the best way to approach this is not to view the external constraint as being a new limitation on policy action; rather it would be folded in with the concern for domestic inflation that is the key limitation on fiscal policy within Functional Finance. The risk of too-loose fiscal policy is still inflation; the debate is whether the external sector provides a significant channel for inflation to develop. Since the influence of the currency on the domestic price level appears weak for developed countries, the weighting of concern should be on domestic developments.

Pinning down the specific weighting between domestic and external inflation risks depends upon complex open economy models. (An open economy model is a model that takes into account more than one country; a closed economy model ignores the rest of the world.) There is little consensus about the form of such a model, unfortunately.

8.6 Sub-Sovereigns

The analysis of sub-sovereign governments, such as municipalities or regional governments like Canadian provinces or American states is beyond the scope of this text. Unfortunately, for these governments, most of the analysis herein is not applicable to them. They are pretty much in the same position as households or corporations. The credit analysis for sub-sovereigns follows different rules than for corporations, but that is not saying a lot. Even within corporate finance, different sectors have wildly different norms for credit. For example, banks routinely have balance sheets with very little equity, which would be completely unacceptable for a mining corporation.

Some analysts might beg to differ, and say that central governments and sub-sovereigns have similar accounting principles and modes of finance. For example, the financial infrastructure around a Government of Canada bond is almost identical to a bond issued by the city of Toronto. However, the key operational differences between a central government and a household that outline within this report also divide a central government from a sub-sovereign.

- The most important is that the central government controls the central bank, and central government bonds are usually the key position-making instrument in the financial system. (Please note the discussion in Appendix 2, where a central government might be superficially similar to other borrowers in an "over-draft economy.")
- The central government is the recipient of "seigneurage revenue," which creates a hedge against higher interest rates.
- The central government has control over the legal infrastructure it borrows in. (Or at least it does if it is sensible.)
- In most cases, sub-sovereign governments are too small to worry about Functional Finance principles. (Canadian provinces are a possible exception to that statement.)
- Central government finances are typically run in a professional fashion, with a well-developed bureaucratic infrastructure. Central government spending is the focus of extreme partisan debate, and it is watched closely by opposition parties. Municipal finance can be run in an extremely amateurish fashion, and this is often done without significant monitoring.

Although these factors make sub-sovereigns closer to corporations, we cannot ignore the role of politics. The central government has the capacity to bail out sub-sovereigns, and to a certain extent, this reality overshadows narrow financial statement analysis. Senior governments are unlikely to step in to bail out an out-of-control small municipality, as there are unlikely to be side effects of the bankruptcy. However, if you are looking at a large government like a central Canadian province, we are in the realm of "too big to fail." The only Canadian provincial default was Alberta in the 1930s, and that was the result of the animosity towards the Social Credit Party by federal politicians. In addition, Alberta was a dirt-poor agricultural province at that time, so there were little economic consequences in the more industrialised Eastern provinces (which dominate federal politics).

8.7 Concluding Remarks

Central governments that impose external constraints upon their currency lose a great deal of their freedom of action. They can be forced to default on these promises, much like corporations and households. That said, governments typically control the legal environment that they borrow in, and may choose to change the constraints rather than stop payments on their bonds. The default that occurs is a breakage between the currency and some external instrument, rather than an interruption of cash flows.

Sub-sovereigns do not control the legal environment that they borrow in, and so they may have no choice but to fail to meet contractual cash flows on their debts. The only real distinction from them and the private sector is that they have a stronger political relationship with the central government, and so judging the risk of default requires more consideration of politics.

Chapter 9 Conclusions

The finances of central governments with free-floating currencies operate in a very distinctive manner. We cannot transfer modes
of thinking used by credit analysts in the analysis of corporations, or even sub-sovereign governments. The decision to default
by such a government is voluntary; the private sector operates within a framework that is defined by the operations of the central bank.

We need to look elsewhere to see what the true limits of fiscal policy are. We need to be able to judge how different policies
will affect growth and inflation. Acceptability of such policies depends upon elected officials, who are ultimately answerable to voters. At present, the political consensus is in favour of relatively tight
fiscal policy that keeps inflation bottled up. This is coming at the cost
of sluggish growth rates and persistently high youth unemployment.

The discussion of these trade-offs brings us away from the basic analysis of governmental balance sheets, towards models of the
economy. Despite decades of research, there have been little advanc-
es made in our ability to forecast the effects of policy changes. At
the same time, all such modelling work is mired in deep political controversy. This type of analysis will be the subject of future reports. I
doubt that I will be able to solve the problem of how to do such forecasts, but I hope to illuminate what the underlying issues are at least.

A.1 Appendix: Government Bonds and Bills

A1.1 Introduction

Government debt largely consists of two types of instruments: short-term Treasury bills, and bonds. Treasury bills typically have a maximum maturity of 12 months at issuance, while bonds have longer maturities. From the point of view of security analysis, the difference is that bonds pay interest in the form of periodic coupons, while Treasury bills only make a payment when they mature. I will henceforth refer to Treasury bills as "bills."

For reasons of space, I will not attempt to cover the details of fixed income mathematics. Doing calculations properly is difficult, as there are precise conventions one needs to follow. The best approach is to use a commercial pricing platform or software library. However, I will now discuss approximate formulas to explain the underlying principles.

A1.2 Treasury Bills

Bills are the easiest instrument to price, as they only make one payment. Once we understand how they work, we can easily move on to other instruments (like bonds), as we can treat the instrument as being a package of bills with different maturities and holdings sizes.

When a bill is auctioned, it is sold in units to the winning bidders in the auction (the *primary market*). Those units can then be sold to other investors later in the *secondary market*. At the maturity of the bill, the government transfers money to the current owners of the bills, paying $1 for each unit held. The number of units we own is known as the *face value* of our holdings. For example, if we own 10,000 units, we say we own bills with a face value of $10,000.

Like equities, we discuss the price of bills in terms of the price of a unit, although for historical reasons bond market prices are typically quotes in terms of the price of 100 units. For example, the quoted price may be $95, which means that the price is $95 for $100 face value, or $0.95 for 1 unit ($1 face value). This quote convention was apparently chosen to cause the maximum confusion in the interfaces of pricing software. I will ignore this convention, and use the simpler convention of a $1 base.

Let us assume that a bill matures in 6 months, and you wish to buy 1 unit:

- If you pay more than \$1, you pay more than what you will receive in 6 months, and so you will end up losing money (a negative interest rate). Textbooks used to say that this would never happen, but we have seen such negative interest rates in Europe and Japan.
- If you pay \$1, you will get back exactly what you paid, and thus receive a 0% return.
- If you pay less than \$1, you receive more than what you paid, and therefore a positive interest rate. The amount by which the price is less than \$1 is termed a *discount*, which gives rise to the term *discounting* in the money market.

The price of a Treasury bill is given by:

$$p = \frac{1}{(1+r)^T},$$

where p is the price, r is the interest rate, and T is the time-to-maturity (in years).

Box 1. Treasury Bill Price

Box 1 gives the simplified formula for the calculation of a Treasury bill price. Note that this is a simplification relative to money market conventions, as the format of the interest rate can change, as well as the means of calculating the period of time until maturity (whether we include weekend days within the day count, *et cetera*). These quote convention differences act as a distraction relative to the underlying mathematics, so they are ignored here.

For relatively low interest rates, if the time to maturity is 1 year, the discount to \$1 is roughly equal to the rate of return. For example, if the rate of return is 4%, the price is \$0.9615 (to 4 decimal places), or very close to a 4-cent discount to \$1. This rule-of-thumb breaks down with higher interest rates (for example, a price of \$0.6667 gives a return of 50%).

Discounts for a fraction of a year are roughly equal to the annualised discount times the fraction of a year. For example, if the rate of return is 4%, and the time-to-maturity is 0.5 (6 months), the price of the bill is \$0.9806 (to 4 decimal places). This is fairly close to \$0.98, which is ½ of the (approximate) discount for 1-year. This rule of thumb breaks down for periods longer than one year, as the cumulative return grows.

Nevertheless, in all cases, the simple rule applies: yield (rate of return) up, price down—and vice-versa.

A1.3 Forwards

The notion of a forward rate is important. We can decompose the rate of interest of a long-maturity bill into two components:

1. the rate on a bill of shorter maturity; and
2. the *forward rate* that covers the period between the maturity of the shorter bill and the original maturity.

Box 2 gives the mathematical relationship between the bill rates, maturities, and the forward rate.

The case where the longer maturity is double the maturity of the shorter bill is simple. The forward has an associated maturity that is equal to the shorter bill, and the forward starts at the maturity date of the shorter bill. For low rates of interest, the longer maturity rate is approximately equal to the average of the short maturity rate and the forward rate.

The forward relationship defined by two Treasury bills (the long maturity bill subscripted by l and the short bill by an s), is given by:

$$\frac{1}{(1+r_l)^{T_l}} = \frac{1}{(1+r_s)^{T_s}} \frac{1}{(1+f)^{(T_l-T_s)}},$$

with r_l (r_s) being the interest rates on the long (short) Treasury bill respectively, T_l (T_s) the time-to-maturity of the long (short) bill (in years), and f is the forward rate spanning the time interval $[T_s, T_l]$.

Box 2. Forward equation

For example, assume that we are looking at a 3-month bill and a 6-month bill. The implied forward is the 3-month rate, starting 3 months forward. If the 3-month rate is 2%, and the 6-month rate is 3%, the forward rate is 4.0098%. This can be verified by:

$$\frac{1}{(1.03)^{0.5}} = \frac{1}{(1.02)^{0.25}} \frac{1}{(1.040098)^{0.25}}.$$

One could interpret this as follows. Let us assume that the central bank uses the 3-month bill rate as a policy target rate. (This is currently not the case in the developed economies, but it is not far from reality.) The present time is assumed to be January. The central bank is setting the 3-month bill rate at 2% (the bill will mature in April). If the 6-month bill rate is at 3%, that implies that the central bank will be targeting a 4% (roughly) bill rate in April (3 months forward). If an investor feels that the 3-month rate will be set at a lower level than that, the investor should buy the 6-month bill.

A1.4 Bonds

A bond is more complicated than a bill, as it has intermediate payments, known as coupon payments. A bond has a fixed coupon, typically denoted c, which is roughly equal to the yield at which it was issued (the coupon amount is typically rounded). The two most common conventions for coupon payments are either annual or semi-annual payments.

1. **Annual payments.** For every $1 face value of the bond held, the bond owner receives $\$c$ every year on the anniversary dates of the bond maturity date (in addition to the $1 prepayment at maturity). There is a final coupon payment at maturity, so the full payment on that date is $\$(1+c)$. For example, if the bond matures on June 1, 2025, the coupon payments are paid on June 1ˢᵗ every year until 2025. (If June 1ˢᵗ is a weekend, then the payment day is adjusted using pre-determined rules.) European bonds, for example German, typically pay annually.

2. **Semi-annual payments.** For every $1 face value held, the bond owner receives $\$c/2$ every six months, coinciding with the anniversary date of the bond (in addition to the $1 principal payment). For example, if the bond matures on June 1, 2025, the bond pays $\$c/2$ on June 1ˢᵗ every year up until 2025, and $\$c/2$ on every December 1ˢᵗ up until 2024 (six months ahead of maturity). Once again, payment dates are adjusted to account for weekends.

The yield on the bond is close to the internal rate of return on the bond, although the market uses conventions that are slightly more complicated.

As an example, take a 1-year semi-annual pay bond with a coupon of 4%, and a rate-of-return of 5%. To determine its price, we look at the value of its cash flows.

1. The first coupon payment of $0.02 in six months is worth $0.0195 (which equals $.02 \times (1.05)^{-0.5}$).
2. The final coupon and principal repayment of $1.02 in one year is worth $0.9714 (which equals $1.02 \times (1.05)^{-1}$).

The sum of these two values is $0.9909, which is the price of the bond. Note that the usual market convention is to express prices for $100 face value, and so this price would normally be quoted $99.09.

To calculate the yield (rate of return) is more complicated, as we need to invert the calculation. The straightforward way to do this is to calculate the price based on an initial guess at the yield, and then keep refining the guesses until the original price is matched. Or more sensibly, use a function in a software library to do the calculation.

A.2 Appendix: Overdraft Economies

The working assumption within this report is that the central bank only owns Treasury bills and bonds. This corresponds to standard practice in the "Anglo" economies (Canada, United States, United Kingdom, and Australia). However, not all central banks operate in this fashion, nor did "Anglo" central banks historically. An alternative framework is for private banks to borrow directly from the central bank, possibly in the form of overdrafts (a negative deposit balance), or by *discounting* their assets (loans or bonds).

A pure "overdraft" economy operates solely without the use of bonds; all credit is in the form of bank loans. This is somewhat approximated by the Continental European economies, where banks are the major source of funding for businesses. North American economies are somewhat mixed; small and medium businesses tended to use bank finance, while larger businesses relied on the bond and equity markets. More recently, specialised financial companies and securitisations have made inroads into areas that were traditionally served by banks. For those who are interested, this type of economy is discussed in greater length Section 4.3.8 in Professor Marc Lavoie's textbook *Post-Keynesian Economics: New Foundations*.

Since my focus here is on government finance, I will only look at the effects on the central bank. If the central bank no longer is purchasing government bonds, the operations I laid out in Chapter 4 no longer apply. Instead, the "position-making instrument" will be central bank lending against private sector assets. This could be done either as discounting or repo operations.

In order to picture the effect, to shift to such a system, the central bank would have to replace all of the government bonds on its balance sheet with private sector financial assets.

Since the central bank does not directly purchase bonds, it appears that it could lose control of government bond and bill yields. However, this appearance is probably misleading, so long as it is possible for the banks to rediscount government bonds and bills at the discount rate. If Treasury bill yields were much higher than the central bank's administered discount rate, banks would arbitrage the bill market by buying them and funding the positions at the discount rate. Therefore, in such an environment, Treasury yields may no longer trade with lower yields than other high quality bond yields, but they should not have much higher yields. Although it appears that private sector would have a greater chance of forming a cartel and refuse to roll government debt, this should be more than balanced by the very effective club that the central bank has poised over the banking system, as described below.

In such a system, the central bank is no longer a refuge for economic theorists, since it operates like a *bank*. Central bank staffing budgets would have to make room for new teams of credit analysts. The central bank would be a major source of funding for the financial system, and taxpayers would not tolerate credit losses. Therefore, the central bank would have to understand the financial firms it is lending to, as well as the assets it is lending against. This is in complete contrast to the position of the central banks during the Financial Crisis, where they had little idea what was happening in the financial system until it was too late. The Fed was even forced to bring in private sector managers to manage the insanely complicated assets it purchased during bailout programmes.

Moving to such a system in the United States was a reform advocated by Hyman Minsky in Chapter 13 of *Stabilizing an Unstable Economy*. His concern was that the financial system has an innate tendency to drift from safe ("hedge") financing schemes towards "speculative" or "Ponzi" financing. If the U.S. Federal Reserve was deeply involved in determining which assets it was willing to lend against, it could act as a countervailing force against this tendency for excessive risk. If it thought a type of lending was unsafe, it could make it ineligible for rediscounting at the central bank. Some specialist lenders may take their chances with such lending, but they would be outside the safety net of the lender-of-last-resort operations. Minsky argued: "Central banks have to steer the evolution of the financial structure."[46]

The fact that the central bank is a major source of funding for the banks in such a system means that "rollover" risk can easily be contained by central bank arm-twisting. It is very difficult for banks to collude against the interests of a major source of their *short-term* funding (as well as the source of their banking license). This means that switching to such a system does not truly create constraints on government finance, but it does require

---

46   Page 359 of *Stabilizing an Unstable Economy*, by Hyman Minsky. Published by McGraw Hill, 2008.

that the central bank bureaucracy be staffed with people who seek to defend the national interest, even at the cost of overriding "market forces."

I agree with Minsky that such a reform would be one of the few mechanisms that would bring some stability to financing arrangements. The catch is that I doubt that such muscular interventions into the banking system fit current political trends. Progressives would be horrified to see the government actively involved in providing financing for *bankers*, while free market advocates would be horrified by the scope of the government interventions. It might require the financial system to blow itself up in an even more impressive fashion to force deep reforms of this nature.

A.3 Appendix: Rate Expectations and the Term Premium

For simplicity, I will assume that the central bank targets the 3-month interest rate. This was the practice at the Swiss National Bank before the financial crisis, so this is not a wildly unrealistic assumption. In the pre-Financial Crisis era, most of the "Anglo" central banks' policy rates were overnight instruments, while the ECB targeted a 2-week refinance rate. However, as I noted in Section 6.4, the policy rate is typically assumed to be unchanged between meetings (other than when emergency rate cuts are seen as necessary). As a result, we end up with a *de facto* policy of the central bank pinning down short rates for a period of time equal to the space between meetings, which is (about) half of the 3-month period I use here. If the reader is a stickler for details, feel free to cut down the time intervals I use by half.

I will also make the additional assumption that the 3-month Treasury bill trades exactly where the central bank target is. Money market traders would object that there are spreads between different money market instruments, which is correct. You would need to adjust the figures I use for an appropriate spread, but this only changes the picture superficially. A more important objection is a potential breakdown in the pricing of government bills and bonds versus the policy rate, which is the subject of Section 6.6 (on rollover risk). This section explains how the fixed income mathematics works in the absence of such a breakdown.

Let us assume that the central bank is targeting[47] a 3-month rate of 1%.[48] We then turn to look at the yield on a 6-month Treasury bill. If the

---

47   Some economists object to the use of the term of "targeting" when discussing an interest rate risk. They prefer a terminology that says that (modern) central bank "targets" something like inflation. In this case, the 3-month Treasury bill yield could be thought of as an "operational target." I prefer to use the term "target" in this case as there is no guarantee that the Treasury bill yield is exactly where the central bank wants it. It can set an administered rate at an arbitrary level, but not a traded instrument.

48   The interest rates used in these examples always end up looking

6-month bill rate is 1.25%, we can then use the forward relationship given in Section A.1.3 to determine the forward rate that is implied by those two bill rates. The forward covers the 3-month period that is between the maturity dates of the 3-month and the 6-month bill, and so is the 3-month rate (6 months less 3 months) starting 3-months forward (after the maturity of the shorter bill). The forward rate is calculated to be 1.5006% (which I will hereafter round off to 1.50%).

This forward rate has a few implications.

- Within a mathematical model of interest rates (such as an option-pricing model), the *expected value* of the 3-month rate, 3 months in the future is 1.50%. (The expected value is a mathematical term, which is the weighted average of the future 3-month rate under the probabilistic scenarios within the model. The weight for each scenario is its probability of occurrence.) If you believe in efficient markets, this expected value should match the everyday meaning of "expectation," which is the consensus forecast of the future 3-month rate. (There is a qualifier about the term premium, discussed later.)
- If you buy a 6-month bill and then finance the purchase with a 3-month term repo (assuming the repo rate is 1% and no "haircut"), the forward price in the repo transaction will be the equivalent of a 3-month bill rate of 1.50%. You will have locked in a cheaper forward price than the market price if the 3-month rate is below 1.50% when the repo expires.
- The 6-month bill will have a higher return than the 3-month bill over the life of the 3-month bill if the future 3-month rate is below 1.50%.
- If you entered into a forward short rate derivative transaction for the 3-month rate, 3-months forward (the equivalent of a Eurodollar future or a forward Overnight Index Swap), the fair value of the derivative is 1.50%.

As can be seen, there are a wide number of trading strategies that would be profitable if the future 3-month rate is below 1.50% in three months (and the opposite trades would be profitable if the future rate is above 1.50%). We will often say that the markets are discounting a

amusing years later.

future 3-month rate of 1.50%. In the real world, these various trades would have slightly different break-even points, which can prove to be disastrous if you are employing a great deal of leverage. Nevertheless, the message of these trades is simple: we should not think of a 6-month bill at 1.25% as a stand-alone instrument, rather a combination of:

1. a 3-month bill with a yield of 1%; and
2. a 3-month bill starting 3 months forward at a yield of 1.5%.

Bond and money market investors (which include bank treasurers) do think this way. When they think about the 6-month bill, they will ask themselves: does it make sense that the 3-month bill rate will be 1.5% in 3 months? (Remember that we are assuming that the central bank is fixing the 3-month rate, and so we can compare that forward rate to what we think the central bank is going to do.) If we think it is unlikely that the central bank will hike rates, the 6-month bill looks like a good buy relative to the 3-month bill. If "everyone" agrees with that assessment, the yield on the 6-month bill would be pushed lower as there would be an imbalance in the market (many buyers willing to buy at that yield versus few sellers).

We can then extend this analysis to the 9-month bill. If it has a yield of 1.50%, we can then back out the forward rate that links it to the 6-month bill (the 3-month rate starting 6 months in the future); the forward rate is 2.0019%. This implies that the market is incorporating the central bank raising rates by about 1% over the next six months.

This analysis can be repeated out as far as we wish. We convert the observed yield curve into a curve that shows the path of forward 3-month rates. One then can decide whether bond yields are too high or too low based on whether we think the central bank will set the 3-month rate higher or lower than the path of the forwards.

One thing to note with this example is that the forward rates are higher than the bill rates. The 9-month bill rate was 1.50%, or 50 basis points above the current policy rate, which translated into a forward rate at 2%, or 100 basis points above the policy rate. Most of the time bond yields are higher than the policy rate, and we see this form of relationship. (When bond yields are below the policy rate, the curve is said to be *inverted*. The implication is that the bond market expects rate cuts from the central bank, which is a sign that the market expects a recession.)

One complication that I have ignored so far is the concept of the *term premium*. A longer maturity bond displays greater price volatility than one of shorter maturity (and thus any losses in market value are greater). Additionally, there is a large imbalance between investors seeking short-term investments versus borrowers willing to borrow with short maturities. This means that there is a pricing bias against long-term instruments, or equivalently, their yields are higher. Therefore, investors should only be willing to buy longer-term instruments if the discounted forward rate is above the forecast path of short rates.

This creates a slight linguistic problem with the use of the word *expected* in analysis. For technical reasons related to how options are priced, the forward rate does correspond to the *expected* rate, which is the result of the calculation of the mathematical expectations operator. We should predict that the forward rate is higher than what investors should *forecast*, which matches the common usage of the word *expected*.[49]

We cannot determine what the term premium is, nor are there reliable model-based estimates. This is because measured bond yields equal the sum of two unmeasured variables: investor rate expectations plus the term premium. That said, it appears safe to say that the term premium for maturities under 2 years is small—around 20 basis points at most. Therefore, the "front end of the curve" tends to track what people forecast the central bank to do, while longer-term bonds are free to swing around more.

The key conclusion for government finance is that the stance of the central bank is key for the determination of bill yields, as well as for short-maturity bonds. How short "short-maturity" is depends on whom you talk to.

---

49   On a technical note, the implication is that this means that the forward rate is not the valid expectation if we are looking at the time series of yields. The forward rate is equal to the expected value only for the "risk-neutral probability measure."

Data Sources

This text relies upon data that has come from a variety of national sources. In some cases, the data are calculated by one agency, but distributed by another. My charts list the data sources used (in abbreviated form).

- **Canada.** Canadian data used was either calculated by Statistics Canada or the Bank of Canada. All data have been downloaded from the CANSIM delivery platform. URL: http://www5.statcan. gc.ca/cansim/home-accueil?lang=eng&p2=50&HPA

- **United States.** The United States has a number of agencies that generate statistical data. I most commonly use the Bureau of Economic Analysis (BEA) as well as the Bureau of Labor Statistics (BLS). For most of these sources, I download the data from the Federal Reserve Economic Data (FRED) web site, which is a service provided by the St. Louis Federal Reserve Bank. (Other sources for U.S. data are noted below.) URL: http://research.stlouisfed. org/fred2/

- **United States Flow of Funds.** This is the Z.1 release, which is calculated by the Board of Governors of the Federal Reserve System. It is a comprehensive database of stocks and flows of financial assets. Given the number of series involved, it is easier to download the entire block of Z.1 data than on a series-by-series basis from FRED. URL: http://www.federalreserve.gov/releases/ z1/

- **IMF.** The IMF publishes World Economic Outlook (WEO) databases, which contains historical data as well as forecasts. One of the advantages of these data is that the data are presented using a consistent set of national accounting concepts. URL: https:// www.imf.org/external/ns/cs.aspx?id=28

- **Japanese Ministry of Finance.** The Ministry of Finance (MoF) has a number of databases, including bond yields. URL: http:// www.mof.go.jp/english/jgbs/reference/interest_rate/index.htm

Calculations and plotting are done in the R computer language. Plots are generated using the *ggplot2* package.

References and Further Reading

References to articles and some books appear within the endnotes of this report. The following books were referred to frequently during the writing of this report. They represent a good starting point for readers who want a deeper understanding of the topics discussed here.

- *Understanding Modern Money: The Key to Full Employment and Price Stability*, by L. Randall Wray, Edward Elgar Publishing, 1998.
- *Seven Deadly Innocent Frauds of Economic Policy*, by Warren Mosler, Valance Co. Ltd., 2010
- *The Stock-Flow Consistent Approach: Selected Writings of Wynne Godley*, edited by Marc Lavoie and Gennaro Zezz, Palgrave Macmillan, 2012.
- *Stabilizing an Unstable Economy*, by Hyman Minsky, McGraw Hill, 2008.
- *Post-Keynesian Economics: New Foundations*, by Marc Lavoie, Edward Elgar Publishing, 2014.

There are a number of other introductions to Modern Monetary Theory, particularly in the form of short articles on the internet. Two books of interest are given below.

- *Diagrams & Dollars: Modern Money Illustrated*, an ebook published by J.D. Alt, 2014. As the title indicates, the book uses diagrams to illustrate concepts. It is written at an introductory level.
- *Modern Money Theory: A Primer on Macroeconomics for Sovereign Monetary Systems*, L. Randall Wray, Palgrave Macmillan (2012). This book by Wray covers many of the topics within this report.

About the Author

Brian Romanchuk founded BondEconomics.com in 2013. It is a web site dedicated to providing analytical tools for the understanding of the bond markets and monetary economics.

He previously was a senior fixed income analyst at *la Caisse de dépôt et placement du Québec*. He held a few positions, including being the head of quantitative analysis for fixed income. He worked there from 2006-2013. Previously, he worked as a quantitative analyst at BCA Research, a Montréal-based economic-financial research consultancy, from 1998-2005. During that period, he developed a number of proprietary models for fixed income analysis, as well as covering the economies of a few developed countries.

Brian received a Ph.D. in Control Systems Engineering from the University of Cambridge, and held post-doctoral positions there and at McGill University. His undergraduate degree was in electrical engineering, from McGill. He is a CFA charter holder.

Brian currently lives in the greater Montréal area.

Index

Also by BondEconomics

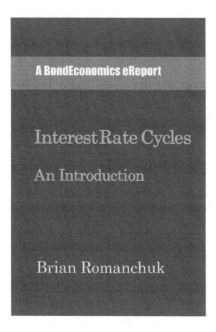

Interest Rate Cycles: An Introduction (June 2016)

Monetary policy has increasingly become the focus of economists and investors. This report describes the factors driving interest rates across the economic cycle. Written by an experienced fixed income analyst, it explains in straightforward terms the theory that lies behind central bank thinking. Although monetary theory appears complex and highly mathematical, the text explains how decisions still end up being based upon qualitative views about the state of the economy.

The text makes heavy use of charts of historical data to illustrate economic concepts and modern monetary history. The report is informal, but contains references and suggestions for further reading.

ISBN Information
ISBN 978-0-9947480-3-4 Epub Edition
ISBN 978-0-9947480-2-7 Kindle Edition
ISBN 978-0-9947480-4-1 Paperback Edition

22318617R00069

Made in the USA
San Bernardino, CA
11 January 2019